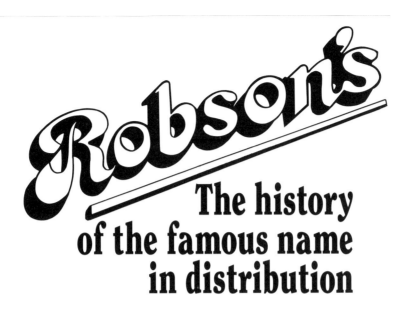

Robson's

The history of the famous name in distribution

BOB TUCK

ROUNDOAK PUBLISHING, NYNEHEAD, WELLINGTON, SOMERSET.

First published in 1990 by
Roundoak Publishing (an imprint of Nynehead Books),
Nynehead,
Wellington,
Somerset,
England TA21 0BX.

© Copyright   **Bob Tuck & Roundoak Publishing**

British Library Cataloguing in Publication Data

Tuck, Bob
    Robsons
    1.   Great Britain, Road freight transport services, history
    I.   Title
    388.3'24

ISBN 1—871565—05—7

Design and typesetting by
Haight Ashbury Design,
Stoke Sub Hamdon,
Somerset.

Printed in Great Britain by
The Amadeus Press,
Huddersfield,
West Yorkshire

Contents

Author's acknowledgements

I must confess that I have been a Robson 'addict' for most of my life. It was thus a great pleasure to be asked by Robert Chicken to develop his idea and original research into this volume of 'Robsons'. However, the transition from being simply a spotter, to that of an historical accountant has only been made possible by the time and assistance proffered by many other Robsons enthusiasts.

The story started with reminiscences from Kitty Robson (Stan's wife), Albert his brother, and Harry Millican, his brother-in-law. Noel O'Reilly (N.T.) gave me a lot of time explaining the business side of Robsons — as well as many other stories of life to boot — and the milk side of operations was recounted by retired drivers George Jackson and Dessy Bright.

George Flenley recalled his input into Robsons and more modern days were explained by Chairman Herbert Nettleship and Managing Director Simon Bellinger. Many other people have helped to fill gaps in the story, two that come straight to mind being old salts Bobby Mawson and David Carr.

But a book of this nature would not have been possible were it not for the wealth of photographic material that many people have allowed to be used in this publication. The main saviour in this area must be the collection of Irvine Millican whose pre-nationalisation shots are close to being priceless. Whilst Peter Davies, Ray Jenkins and Len Foster have given great help, it is Roger Kenney's camera which has also been of huge help in freezing the action of the 1950s and 1960s when the fleet of Robsons were growing.

Many others have helped both with photographs and information, but, after my wife Sylvia, the main stalwart continues to be Geoff Milne whose unselfish attitude and unending patience has helped to smooth this book on 'Robsons' into print.

Stan Robson was not a man who ever enjoyed having to speak in public. Perhaps this book goes a little way in speaking for a Company which he, and many others created, which as well as providing a transport service, gave pleasure to many Robson followers.

Bob Tuck

Foreword

by Robert Chicken

'Robsons' is a history that had to be written. I believe the Company to be one of a select few road haulage operators who have operated for the last six decades, but at the same time, set and maintained increasingly high standards in order to fulfill the demands for distribution requirements of British business and industry.

Bob Tuck's work is a fine tribute to young Stan Robson who set about building a small transport concern. It is an illuminating account of how he saw those early dreams crumble. It relates the rebuilding of the Company leading to nationalisation and the start up again thereafter. It gives a vivid account of how and why the Company was able to expand, thanks to its foward thinking, original policies and attention to market forces. His account is graphically illustrated by a galaxy of photographic and pictorial material, much of which has never been published before.

Robsons has always been a special company in its field because of its individuality and service. It has a core of large and small loyal customers, a host of long serving employees and is a Company whose fleet has, for years, been revered by a huge number of lorry enthusiasts.

I believe that this accurate historical account will be of great interest and value to anyone remotely connected with transport.

The Model T Ford — not this particular one — started Stan Robson, like many others of that era, off into his transport life in 1925. The T had a strange form of transmission where pedal pressure enhanced a variable type of gearbox. The one obvious difference to a 1920s T in use with the preserved 'Veteran' — with Albert Robson behind the wheel — was that treaded tyres, never mind a spare, were a definite luxury.

CHAPTER ONE

In the beginning there was Royalty

It's almost impossible to explain. Why should an obscure town in North West England still have such a magnetic appeal? Why is it that even though they are now counted in their hundreds the sight of one approaching makes your heart miss a beat? It's only a lorry, but why must you try and read the name proudly emblazoned across the front? Why is it that the most level headed of coldly calculating businessmen spent hours discussing it, only to decide that the name of Robson just meant too much to discard? Why did they insist that even though it may be right to drop a 30 year old livery in favour of a more modern look, that an individual name based on a 50 year old whim must still take pride of place on the front of their workhorses?

If you know the answer to these questions you might be able to explain the success that lay ahead of Stan Robson when he was born at Moss Head in 1906. Situated north of Hadrians Wall and yet south of the Scottish border, the hamlet lay in the lee of the Pennines as they drifted down towards the Solway Firth.

Even in the early 1900s pillaging, or politely put, sheep stealing, was still practised, although young Stan — in the middle of a family of three other brothers and three sisters had little thoughts of history as he trudged the five miles every day into Hethersgill.

Describing it as a town may have been slightly overgenerous, but with Carlisle being some 12 miles away, Hethersgill had to be very much self contained. The local school was Stan's daily destination and although it's rural catchment area spread fairly large, the school wasn't that big that you didn't know — albeit only by sight — all the rest who were pressed into attending. One year older was Kathleen Millican, and although she was a girl her claim to fame was that her father ran one of the first motorised charabancs to be doubled up and used as the Post Bus.

Every morning the vehicle had to be in to Carlisle by 5.45 a.m. to collect the mail and working a beat that headed north east, it dropped off the post at Houghton, Scaleby, Smithfield and all the small villages out to Roadhead in the shadow of the Bewcastle fells. The post was collected on a return run every evening, so rare though it might have been, the Millican charabanc was famous throughout this Cumberland backwater.

Young Robson stuck it out at school until he was 13 but the three years following he spent working on the land was merely a stop-gap before he got his first taste of driving. True, you could only ride a motor bike at the age of 16, but the die was cast and the motoring life was to be one for Robson.

Millican Senior sensed the young lad had something about him and even though he was under age and it might not have been strictly legal, he was asked to work the charabanc. Solid tyres, only a sheet of canvas for a roof, but with seats for all who wanted to ride and it was far quicker than walking, if almost more bumpy than horseback. Why he did it no one knows, but for some reason Millican had proudly painted the name of 'Border Queen' on this Hethersgill miracle and the words were to stick in the mind of the impressionable Robson.

By 1925 Stan had gradually built himself a stake which he invested in a weathered Ford Model T saloon car. He

'Border Queen' has always been regarded as the real turning point in Robsons' success, being the first lorry to carry one of the romantic Border names. Her maiden journey on 9th December 1937 was not so romantic as she was towed home by an older Bedford. This aside, Robson's first new Foden went on to give sterling service and was always one of Stan's particular favourites. Pictured here some 11 years old, HH 9783 was one of only a handful of six wheelers run by the Company.

had no intention of using it as Henry Ford had intended, but carrying out a Cumbrian conversion, the back two seats were chopped out and some bits of wood attached. Hardly an excuse for a pick-up truck but the first seed of Robson's haulage enterprise was boldly sown.

If the vehicle was best described as modest, its traffic wasn't much better as Stan contracted himself out to the local council on road construction work. What Cumberland tracks may have suited the traditional horse and cart was no good at all for the new generation of motor cars, but Robson shovelled, carried and filled roadstone into all the nooks and crannies that the council directed in order to build the roads up to scratch. It was to be rather fitting that these same Robson built roads were to be used by Stan as his 'Border' fleet grew.

By 1927 Stan felt confident enough in life to ask for the hand of Kathleen Millican in marriage and on 6th January they vowed a contract which was to last unbroken for more than 59 years. Living in 'Club House', a cottage at Hethersgill, Stan blessed Kitty with all his worldly goods — which meant the Model T — provided she lent a hand in its maintenance. The vehicle's open top garage was the house's back garden and with the cylinder head removed to the kitchen table, the new Mrs. Robson leant the practised craft of grinding valves in, very soon into her married life.

Road making started at 6 am. every day, base of operations being the village of Fenton just east of Carlisle and nine miles from Hethersgill. The Robson team's dedication to preventive vehicle maintenance meant the Ford never missed

a day and Stan was rewarded with more work to employ three more vehicles and drivers.

The growing fleet - which saw a solid tyred Albion and a Bedford join the T - were even to be adorned with the owners name as the Hethersgill kitchen doubled up yet again as a paint shop. The side boards were unhooked from the vehicle's body, brought indoors, and by cutting out a rather crude form of cardboard stencil, the name of S. Robson was hand painted through, onto the woodwork.

Robsons started to feel the cup of a prosperous business was in their hands but just as they lifted it up to drink deeply from it, the cup was dashed from their grasp. The council road surveyor Bill Bowes had tears in his eyes. "The Labour has stopped it all" he told young Robson, but Stan found the actions of the newly elected Labour Government of 1931 almost impossible to believe so far away in the distant capital. "They are bound to start up on road work again," was all that Bob could promise but the weeks drifted by, still with the drivers kept on full pay yet Robson unable to get them any work to do. The situation just couldn't last and reluctantly they were paid off and the vehicles sold on. More truthfully they were almost given away as the recession also had its effect on the second hand lorry business. Whilst Stan hung onto the Model T, the last of his vehicles to go was the solid tyred Albion which Stan took three months in persuading Porters Foundry of Carlisle to give him £25 for. It was to be the best money that the engineering company ever spent, for converted on to pneumatic tyres that lowly priced Scottish built load carrier was used on delivery work for the next 25 years.

Not actually carrying a length of hedge, 'Border Prince' is pictured in Durranhill Road, the four wheeler being an OG Foden which dates from 1939. These OGs were only rated for about a 6 ton payload, although many of their operators — Robsons included — found the little four cylinder Gardner engines well capable of taking another ton of paying cargo in their stride. Isaac 'Ike' Ostle was a regular driver before Freddie Steel took the vehicle over.

'Border Laddie' like early vehicles 'Prince' and 'Princess' all share a Cheshire style of registration number. They were in fact registered and taxed by Fodens so when collected new from the factory they could go straight out to work — normally direct to the mills at Liverpool — so their run back to base at Carlisle wasn't done unladen. Robsons even sent Foden some tins of paint so the manufacturer could paint them in the style required, again, before delivery.

'Border Baron' was the first eight wheeler to come onto fleet, it being bought second hand about 1943. The 1936 ERF was recalled rather strangely as being fitted with the 5 cylinder Gardner engine, rather than the normal six pot version. Its greatest claim to fame was in hauling Robsons biggest load — a huge military gun — from Eskmeals in Cumbria down to Bradford. Crew for this job being driver Tommy Robson and mate George Jackson.

Robson detested the air of despondency that threatened to slowly engulf his life and so decided to tackle it head on. Selling up the cottage at Hethersgill, Stan, Kitty and their young daughter Gladys moved up to Carlisle, their new home at 77, Ashley Street, near the Infirmary, being semi-detached to a butchers shop. Whilst this new house didn't have much of a garden or rural outlook, it did have a garage round the back. In here, starting out with two doors he acquired, Stan and his eldest brother Tommy set to and built a wagon between them.

The chassis and running gear came from a Reo 15 seater bus and although the large exposed radiator was recognisable as coming from a big yankee job, the rest of the cab and bonnet was a one-off Carlisle special. Whilst perhaps fleet of foot with a few lightweight passengers aboard, once the Reo was converted to haulage it changed like Jekyll and Hyde. True, Robson would probably put six ton on its back, but in the early 1930s lorry capacity as far as weight was concerned was very much a 'see what it will carry' type of situation. Braking performance with that sort of weight was close to non existent. The Reo had a form of exposed brake drum that had an outside band running round it and although suitably lined up in the morning, there was no guarantee that it would stop you by the same afternoon. This fancy braking system was very much ornamental and of far more use was a huge stone or Cumbrian 'clemmy' that the mate would throw under the wheel as the only assured way of preventing undesired movement.

The Robson Reo tended to be double manned regularly, not only to make sure someone was available to operate this parking brake but also to help in the standard method of loading known as handballing. Plaster in bags was a regular outward bound load to Darlington, Middlesbrough and York. Coming home meant a load of cattle feed in slab form from the British Oil & Cake Mills (BOCM) of Selby destined for customers of Joe Nixon's concern Border Farmers — fodder suppliers to the farmers in the Carlisle area — he was Stan's first real business colleague.

Driving the Reo was an art in itself. Braking just had to be done by the gearbox and hill climbing anything steep at all was normally done using the lowest gear of all, that of reverse. Learning this technique the hard way was Harry Millican, one of Kitty's younger brothers, who came into the business as soon as his age would allow it. Most of the Robson/Millican family helped out at one time or another with the vehicle, all of Stan's brothers were to drive for him and even Stan's father — always known as 'Fad' — was to later drive one of the Ford vans as the Robson approach to their single vehicle operation was one of maximum utilisation.

Working night and day was described by Albert Robson who said that Stan may have given you a time to start but he rarely gave you a time to finish. The hairy antics of the Reo created enough capital to invest in a Bedford, this being supplied by the S.M.T. dealership in Goldergate, Carlisle, although the pattern of traffic still meant Selby was almost the second home of the Robsons crew. When in Carlisle, Albert and Harry stayed with Stan and Kitty in Ashley Street, the house also doubling up as the company office which took the form of a roll top desk positioned in a corner of the living

'Border Princess' was one of the stronger DG versions of Foden four wheeler and dates from 1938. Robsons had a couple of different systems of removing these demountable bodies, the most novel of which saw them adopt a set of wooden rollers. This allowed the van body to be pushed off onto a specially built dock that had been built to match the height of the four wheeler.

This type of petrol engined Albion, which were not converted to diesel, were usually run by Robsons on milk work out of Carlisle or even handed down to drivers at Gilsland for the same type of low mileage work. 'Border Chief' came to Robsons about 1942 although its grand headlamps are obviously not wartime issue.

room. Looking after what books existed was Jack Barnes who also lived in the Robson house, and when her mother was ill young Gladys can recall that Jack cooked her breakfast one day before going to school — Barnes obviously cooked in a similar manner to which he kept the books, for Gladys recalls that her vivid impressions of the occasion was how thinly he was able to cut the toast.

Whilst many would have thought that it must have been very pleasant to have all your family eventually working alongside you, Stan Robson's attitude was that he always expected that much more from you simply because you were family. Doing her best to keep the physical side of the family drivers fully fuelled, Kitty Robson spent most of her free time baking bread. A large Carrs biscuit tin was standard issue and each was filled to the brim with sandwiches whenever the workers got back to Carlisle. The drivers tended to eat on the run although both Albert Robson and Harry Millican recalled the biscuit tin was normally empty by the time they reached Carleton, which was only a couple of miles south of Carlisle down the A6 as they ravenously devoured the tin's contents, as the Bedford clattered on at a steady 35mph.

The northern cross Pennine journey was the life blood of the Robson business. Going in for plaster to be hauled over to the North East, the Robson vehicle was that regular that they were given a key and told to help themselves so they could run in and out no matter what the hour. Occasionally it may have been a load of rags and woollen that stood high above the headboard on the delivery down to Leeds. Run over to BOCM at Selby or perhaps Ray Anderson at Hull for cattle feed or fish

meal from the factory next door — never a driver's favourite due to the smell — the Bedford was loaded to its maximum for the ride back over the northern hills. Although there was nothing ever put in writing, the Robson men were normally expected to unload the cattle feed up into the highest part of the farmer's loft before delivery would be accepted. It was this part of the job that not only took the longest amount of time but also stuck in the drivers' gullets the most. If the farmers rubbed them up the wrong way it was normally a case of just grinning and bearing it although in time there was a trick or two where Albert or Harry could get their own back.

As long as they did it right, they could normally gauge it so the stacked feed leaned over towards the incoming trap door. The last stack of sacks were placed to lean out even further, they being held up in position by a broom shank or the like. By tying a piece of string to this shank, once the trap door was dropped shut the string could be pulled to remove the steadying broom shank and the pile of sacks were made to accidentally collapse on the trap door and so make it impossible to lift open.

For working all the hours that God sent, Albert remembers that he got paid 10/- (50p) a week, his keep when he was at Carlisle, and all the sandwiches his bait tin could carry. By the end of the week he was often down to his last twopence and if it was a choice between a cup of tea or a twopenny Woodbine, the cigarette usually won because it lasted longer. Sunday was usually a day of rest, but the brain worked overtime as you tried to fill out the newly introduced log sheets (records of daily work) so that they legally showed what

Border Transport (Brampton) Ltd was the Company title that was created to run the two ERF four wheelers that were bought in 1944. Seen loaded with sacked potatoes, CRM 365 tipped the scales unladen at 3 ton 18cwt. 2qtrs, being first registered to John A. Pratt & Sons of Greenhill, Brampton, on 30th November 1937. It was Pratt's two sons who stayed on to drive these two four wheelers after they were sold. Sister vehicle to 'Sailor' being a similar ERF Reg. No. EAO 475 named 'Border Soldier'.

you had been doing all week, and you prayed you hadn't been spotted in a silent check by one of the Ministry men.

As the Robson men's dedication to sheer hard work began to pay off, Stan was able to expand his operations by buying two more Bedfords. Still not new ones, but having been refurbished by S.M.T. they were the best that could be afforded. The type of work they were involved in was quite demanding, as Robson had won work by giving a unique type of service; a Robson trademark for years to come.

Jim Kitching, who was employed by Oliver & Snowdon during the 1930s, recalled that his company of agricultural merchants used Stan Robson to collect loads of feeding stuffs from Liverpool, Hull or Selby. The pattern of the work meant that the merchant's representatives rang in their orders to the office during the afternoon. The mill was contacted and an order placed there, which meant that Stan Robson was rung about 5 p.m. with details what was to be collected and from where. Jim Kitching recalled that without fail the Robson wagon would be in Carlisle with that load at 7 a.m. the next morning waiting to unload. The rates for the job, Jim recalls, was 7/- (35p) per ton, so pushing on 5 ton to the 3 ton Bedfords meant a gross income of 35/- (£1.75) for the overnight haul.

With Tommy, Sid and Albert all having their own Bedfords, things were again starting to look up in 1935, but what seemed like another bomb-shell arrived on the door mat in the guise of an income tax demand that would have bled the shell shocked Robson dry.

More than happy whilst delving into, or under, one of

With the adaptation of removable rather than fixed van bodies, Stan Robson gave his vehicles more versatility even if the containers tended to look a bit weathered. 'Border Maiden', a petrol engined Albion, Reg. No. HHT 147, sports the same box that is seen later on 'Border Airman'.

'Border King' sports typically austere wartime issue headlamps as it came new to Robsons on 24th August 1944. Big lad Cyril Steele, the Foden's regular driver, took a lot of pride in the vehicle, which at the time was the natural fleet flagship. Seen sporting new sheets, these were made by George Sewell in his warehouse at East Tower Street, Carlisle.

George Jackson is pictured in August 1944 in one of the ex Laidlaw Bedfords that formed part of Border Hauliers (Gilsland) Ltd. Seen near Greenhead, the Bedford is carrying a set of milk cans but the large dropside bodywork also allowed the vehicle to carry many loads of coal. This was carried from Venters Hall Pit to Carlisle Power Station, but with no tipping gear, unloading was done by driver and shovel.

his wagons, Stan was never particularly at ease with paperwork, preferring to conduct his business in a more direct, perhaps even old fashioned way, with the shake of a hand and the handling of cash. Not knowing exactly what to do with this non-descript buff form, he was introduced to N.T. O'Reilly, a man who had just set up on his own as an Accountant. Although haulage contractors were sometimes thought of as dirty words in the accountancy trade — because they always seemed to be going bust — Noel Thomas O'Reilly (always referred to as N.T.) was at the infancy of his career and any client was deemed to be far better than no clients at all.

It was a simple matter for N.T. to inform Stan how to make an appeal against the income tax Inspector's findings, and with this small gesture, Robson and O'Reilly forged a relationship that bridged both business and friendship which was to remain unbroken for more than 50 years. N.T. readily admitted that he knew nothing about lorries, but he was more than conversant in the ways that a business must be run. Over the months that were to follow he soon appreciated that Robson knew his onions in transport, so when it came round to formalising this developing business connection, both Robson and O'Reilly had built up faith in each other.

It was in 1936 that O'Reilly suggested that Robson should do something that seemed rather dramatic. "Form a limited company" he told Stan, "and if you do happen to fold then you aren't responsible for any debts that the company may accrue." Robsons (Hauliers) Ltd. may not have been a very imaginative title to adopt but it gave Stan a sense of credibility as well as a brass plate to admire. With O'Reilly

First registered to William Mackenzie, 78 Shaddow Gate, Carlisle, on 11th October 1935, chassis no. 90064 had an unladen weight of 1 ton 18cwt. 1qtr. 7lbs. Robsons used this Bedford for a very early form of distribution in that working for the Carlisle based 'Red Stamp Store', it used to deliver weekly grocery orders around the Carlisle area. If not driving it, Stan's father — usually known as 'Fad' — would be riding as passenger and navigator. The vehicle was last taxed in 1953 and scrapped in 1956.

Whilst the total acceptance of road tankers for milk haulage was to see Robsons leave the churn work in the early 1970s, the company were in fact running tankers for that type of traffic nearly 30 years earlier. First registered on 19th January 1946, 'Border Monarch' was driven at times by Tommy Pratt but in the main by Adam Stevens. Its main haul was taking milk from the Border Dairy in Carlisle to the Western Dairy in Newcastle.

eventually agreeing to accept a directorship in the concern, it also meant a great deal of peace of mind to Robson in an area of his business which he admitted wasn't his best. What Stan was to excel at was in the practical application of making the best of day to day purchases and general business acumen.

Looking at the transport business of Robsons through an accountant's eyes, N.T. soon identified two particular problems. The lightweight, second-hand Bedfords were not carrying enough payload — even with far more aboard than their manufacturer envisaged — plus they were costing a mint in spare parts and maintenance costs. The solution to the problem was to get some bigger lorries able to carry far more but also ones that were brand new.

Of all the lorry builders in production during the mid 1930s, Robson felt that the reputation of engineering, strength and reliability shown by Foden was second to none. But even with his fellow director O'Reilly alongside him, it was still a nervous drive down to Sandbach in Stan's black sedan where they asked for and were granted an audience with Mr. William.

Whilst the fortunes of Stan Robson had fluctuated wildly in the previous 12 years, it was nothing when compared to the trauma befalling Foden Ltd. In 1924 Mr. William Foden, eldest son of the company founder, Edwin Foden, had severed all links with the company and emigrated with his family to take up farming in Australia. Whilst his younger brother Edwin Richard (always known as E.R.) stayed on with Fodens, although with total disatisfaction with the way that the Foden board was running the business. It eventually came to a head in the early 1930s when E. R. resigned and with his son Dennis

created the lorry building concern of E.R.F. as direct competition, being right on the Foden doorstep in Sandbach.

The dissent amongst these Foden elders all revolved round the Foden Board's insistence that Steam was still very much 'King' and they showed little inclination whatsoever to develop diesel powered lorries until the law makers rang the death knell of steamers due to over taxation. As Foden slid towards bankruptcy and oblivion, a cry for help was sent to the southern hemisphere. More by curiosity Mr. Willy called into Sandbach whilst on a European holiday, but the brief glimpse of impending doom was enough to make him return to Cheshire for good. Taking up the role of Managing Director designate, his influence was enough to immediately turn Fodens round, step up the diesel powered development and within a couple of years present the new DG range of Foden vehicles, which many people believed were the most superior vehicles of their time.

As well as an exceptional degree of business acumen, Mr. Willy had an exceptional insight into people and grasping the hand of the 30 year old from Cumberland he forged a link that Stan Robson kept with Foden until 1980 and Mr. Willy retained with Robson until he died in 1964.

The actual business of the sale was conducted with Ted Foden, Mr. Willy's elder son who had been given the sales brief in the 'new look' Foden. Whilst Robson was keen to buy and Foden keen to sell, to make an impression in the Carlisle area, the only problem was one of payment. Stan had actually decided upon a 'Chinese Six' twin steer six wheeler which was far lighter in unladen weight than a conventional double drive

six wheeler and so could carry a lot more payload within the legal six wheeler's limit of 18 ton then in force. Stan was restricted in getting anything bigger, for the 'A' carrier's licence he had to transfer on to the new Foden also put a limit to its unladen weight written into the licence.

Stan had always had his own thoughts on the Chinese Six. With four wheels on the front it gave you safer steering capacity, and should you happen to have a blow out on the back end, you could always borrow one of the four on the front and still get away with things. Noel O'Reilly recalls that between him and Stan that day they hardly had a £1 in cash but the figure they were discussing for payment for the Foden was £1400. Ted Foden actually agreed to come up to Carlisle to inspect their proposed 'trade-in', a Leyland Cub four wheeled tipper of questionable years. As a means of diversification away from agricultural feed traffic Robson had worked this little tipper on moving gravel from a bed at Longtown. N.T. felt the weathered Leyland was worth in the region of £50 so when Ted Foden offered them £250 they naturally couldn't accept the deal quick enough.

Up to Carlisle the new Foden had a platform body fitted and a two tone paint job in red. At the time HH 9783 was the pinnacle of the Robson haulage career, as far as Stan was concerned it was his Queen, and in expensive gold leaf he adorned it with the name from that long gone Millican chara-banc, 'Border Queen'. No great plan, no hidden philosophy, it just seemed like a good idea at the time to name it, but yet another die was cast and the most famous hallmark of the Robson tradition was made. 9th December 1937 was the day

the Queen took to the road, memorable, but perhaps not over impressive, because of the cold. Stan's two elder brothers Sid and Tommy were to leave Carlisle at midnight for an empty run over to Selby and though she was a lot more noisy than the Bedford, the Queen was elegance personified and the Robson men felt as though they were on the throne of haulage.

Handballing a load of cattle cake in slab form onto the Queen's back didn't take over long so she was soon able to show her paces over the terror that was Stainmoor, the bleak stretch of moor between Scotch Corner and Penrith. She felt a bit tight but that was only natural as she was still brand new, but on the run up from Penrith at High Heskett, in Cumbrian terms "she just laid down". Translated this meant she stopped as the engine cried enough.

It was almost degrading having to tranship the load from a brand new vehicle onto another vehicle. After the Foden had been towed home by a Bedford, the fault under the bonnet was diagnosed as a seized impeller pump. This seemed strange as the Gardner diesel engine was renowned for it's very cold running temperature. Even climbing the likes of Shap could be done without any water if you took it steady, whilst many Gardner engines ran without any form of fan blade, a trick that might save a little on power loss for a device that was totally unnecessary. Whilst a low temperature engine might have been hell for a driver freezing in his cab, it did mean for little wear in the internal heart of the engine, with a long life being a Gardner engine guarantee, one reason why Robson, like many others, specified them every time they could.

First day's work apart 'Border Queen' was to be a tremendous servant for the Robson fleet. Total reliability, brakes that could work and all the Gardner horses working long and hard. Stan recalled it was to be 10 years on before the Gardner could be stripped down, although all that half a million miles had done was to create two thousandths of an inch of wear on the crankshaft. To formalise a base of operations for the newly bought Foden, Stan purchased an old Post Office yard on Durranhill Road in the Harroby area of Carlisle which had started out in life as Young's riding school. Across the road, also in Durranhill Road, was the depot of Thistle Transport, a general haulage concern owned by the transport company of Alexander Smart from Leith, albeit run as a separate entity. Manager at Thistle was a Mr. McGillvery and although Robsons weren't of a size to worry the mighty Smart/Thistle organisation — yet — Stan settled in to be at least reasonable competition.

The fleet expanded at a healthy rate with new Fodens arriving in 1938 and 1939. Only four wheelers, but in 'Border Princess' and 'Border Prince', were the natural descendants of that first 'Queen'. Albert Robson got a new vehicle in the 'Princess' but his time with it was short lived as with World War II breaking out, he was called up for Army service and Bobby Mawson was given the keys of this relatively new Foden in 1940. It was obvious that when it did arrive some years later, 'Border King' was to be an eight wheeler, a size and stature befitting of its name.

Bobby recalls that at that time there were seven vehicles in the fleet. Along with the royal named Fodens was another new Foden four wheeler 'Border Laddie', apparently named after Stan's dog, whilst two old tippers, a Guy and a Bedford, were worked hard on gravel work out of Longtown. Making up the numbers was an old petrol engined Albion four wheeler used on milk collection.

With many vehicles being totally commandeered to fight the war effort, Stan Robson also found his four premium Fodens were detailed to be used in the M.O.W.T. - Ministry of War Transport structure. In essence this meant government management of long distance road haulage, similar to the later nationalisation, albeit under local controllers. It was like rubbing salt in the wound when Stan heard that the local controller of his vehicles was neighbour McGillvery of Thistle Transport, but it did mean very regular work and pay for the driving staff, although when compared to today's wages they seem pitifully small.

A look at Bobby Mawson's pay chit dated 10th April 1942 shows that his hourly rate was 1s.8d. (about 8½p). The 51 hour week was only swelled to reasonable proportions as the three extra hours were paid at time and an eighth, plus Good Friday working added another 16s. 9½d (about 84p). Deductions also made interesting reading for along with 5s.4d. Income Tax and 1s.0d. National Insurance, there was a hefty 1s.3d (6½p) taken off for cleaning your overalls.

On top of their normal wages the drivers also got their overnight money which at this time was about 2s.6d. per night (12½p). Regular trips were made down country with cargoes ranging from bacon to lead ore. The bacon was hauled from Cavaghan & Grays in Carlisle for rationed distribution

'Border Empress' is one of the many fine sounding names that continue to be used more than 40 years on from their original inception. This small DG Foden was the first recipient of the name, it taking to the road on 24th June 1946. Regular driver at this time was Stan Clifford. The vehicle is seen at base, fully loaded with faggots. Robsons did this job on a sub contract basis from Jos Millican of Penton, collecting the off cuts of timber from Newcastleton for onward delivery into Lancashire.

The invoice/ specification in respect of 'Border Empress' makes for interesting reading. Over two years to wait and only 5% discount, but thankfully, an electric starter.

TELEGRAMS FODENWAY SANDBACH   TELEPHONE SANDBACH 44 (5 lines) EXTN. No.

M ess . Robsons Hauliers (Carlisle)Ltd.,
The Garage,
Durran Mill Road,
Carlisle.

Bought of **FODENS LIMITED**

Foden
EST 1856

ELWORTH WORKS SANDBACH
CHESHIRE

COMMERCIAL & PASSENGER VEHICLES
PIONEERS OF THE FODEN STEAM WAGON   22nd June   1946.
GB.

Your Order No.   Cases will be allowed in full if returned in good order. Carriage Paid.   Per

Date   Carr.

1	New Foden Diesel DG4/7 Ton Standard Chassis and Cab No.25178, fitted with Gardner 4 Cylinder L.W.Engine fitted with Electric Starter, four speed and reverse super low gearbox, standard axle ratio, studdisc pattern wheels fitted with 36 x 8 H.D.Tyres, single fronts, twin rears, spare wheel and tyre, semi-streamline saloon pattern cab, 32 Gallon fuel tank, front and spring pattern rear pulling jaws, Simms Electric Lighting and Starting Equipment including Foglamp, and complete outfit of tools and accessories as per your order dated 12th April 1944.	1528	0	0
	Less 5% Discount	:76	0	0
	NETT.	£1452	0	0
	Delivery charges	4	.	
		£1456	-	
	Delivery Ex Works. Nett Cash when ready for delivery			

CODE A.B.C 5TH EDITION

Perhaps better recognised from the theatre of war, Robsons took delivery of this ex W.D. Daimler in crated form about 1945 and built it up at their own workshops. Some remarkable tales are told of this petrol engined four wheel drive powerhouse, which ran on trade plates, especially when fitter Geoff Young was at the wheel. Even 22 tons of loaded eight wheeler was easily hauled at the end of a straight bar, either up or down the likes of Shap. 'Border Warrior' passed to BRS with the majority of the fleet on nationalisation, but when the Carleton depot fitted twin tyres to the rear axle, the Daimler never seemed to have the same level of performance.

When compared to Jock Straiton's 'Border Lady', Robsons second Bedford artic 'Border Duchess' seems particularly elegant. This petrol engined mount took to the road on 19th September 1946, it being coupled to a Scammell made semi-trailer. Both the artics sported the twin forks type coupling but rarely, it was recalled, did the tractor units uncouple their individual trailers. Regular driver was Davey Coulthard who could handle his bendy vehicle like his expertise with darts, for he was a man who would never miss 'Double Top'.

round Preston, Lancaster and Manchester. Contrasting in the extreme was lead ore powder hauled from mine works not far from Lake Ullswater at Glenridding. Quite a devil of a traffic which had to be loaded by hand for a single shovelfull could weigh close to 56lbs.

Getting new lorries during the War was out of the question but one vehicle which was new to Robsons that came during the early 1940s and was to receive the name of 'Border Baron' was remembered because it was so old. It came to Carlisle painted in green with the name of an operator from Sandy, Bedfordshire painted on its rusting remains. But the 'Baron's' greatest claim to fame was how it was involved in the hauling of Robsons biggest war time load, a huge artillery gun which was taken from Eskmeals on the Cumberland coast down to Bradford.

Prior to starting the haul, driver Tommy Robson went into High Duty Alloys at Workington where he was given a huge metal casting to act as ballast on the back of the 1936 ERF eight wheeler, Reg. No. DMA 756. The gun proved to be of little problem to Tommy, although driver's mate George Jackson possibly had the hardest job for the entire descent down from Shap summit on the A6 saw him sat astride the gun hauling on the small handbrake.

Whilst 'Border Queen' went to Northern Ireland to run spares and equipment to the first American camps on this side of the Atlantic, other Border vehicles went to Liverpool and assisted in night time evacuations to safer areas. Get caught in a raid and the driver had to leap out and crawl underneath to use the huge Foden presence as a form of physical protection. Another war time incident recalled, revolved around Stan's love of his Border fleet and his ability to identify them even by just listening to the sound of their engines.

Lying in bed one night Kitty woke up about 4 a.m. to find Stan wide awake. "What's the matter?" she asked. "Well, if I didn't know that the 'Princess' was safely parked in the garage, I would have said that was her," indicating to the sound of a noisy diesel engine fading into the distance. Stan and Kitty lived on the main A6 highway at 254 London Road and passing traffic at all hours especially during the war, was a regular occurrence. "Go back to sleep", she said rather crossly, but next morning it was discovered that "Border Princess" and its van load of antique furniture had been stolen from the depot during the night and Stan had not been imagining things.

'Princess' was eventually recovered after she was found abandoned with her clutch burnt out on the fells near Caldbec, but with her precious load still intact. Nothing underhand was intended apart from a deserting soldier trying to abscond from a nearby Army camp in Durranhill Road, he having taken the Foden out of Robsons merely as a quick form of get away vehicle.

Although Stan later recalled that the company never lost a single item during the war, he, like the rest of the country, breathed a deep sight of relief as 1945 dawned with hard-fought for peace finally being achieved. But, if the last six years had been a form of hell for the country, then it was to be the next six years which were to be hell for this man.

The two shots (left and below) of 'Border Emperor' reflects the before and after effects of paint applied by the expert hand of Jimmy Hornsby. The face behind the wheel is that of Ted Leighton. Like Hornsby, Ted was an avid football supporter and was to almost get his cards by preferring to go and watch a big match rather than follow orders to load his wagon. Note should be made in how the ERF received its fleet lettering of ERFO rather than in a fashion similar to every other marque on fleet.

'Border Knight' is one of the ex Thistle Albions being first registered on 18th July 1940. The vehicle is fully loaded with sold surplus equipment out of one of the two Ministry of Defence posts near to Carlisle. The M.U. at Kingstown and C.A.D. at Longtown could be visited by Robsons vehicles every day but the fleet drivers said that security was that tight it was probably easier to get into Fort Knox.

Joe Bell is seen at the wheel of the ex Thistle 'Border Lassie' which ran out of Carlisle on churn work under the banner of Border Deliveries Ltd. The petrol engined Albion dates from 26th November 1937, its area of collection being the farms round Cotehill and Armathwaite, which is south of Carlisle. Joe is recalled as also having a second 'afternoon' job which was erecting marquees at large shows and events in the area.

CHAPTER TWO

Held together by milk

The mid 1940s was a difficult time for life in general. There was still the rationing and shortages that wartime hostilities had inflicted, but the euphoria of peace meant feelings and attitudes could be mixed. If anything, road transport was now even more important as the shakedown towards normality took place, although the wartime years hadn't prevented Stan Robson in slowly enlarging his road going fleet, it being more a case of being egged on by his customers.

In the main these acquisitions had been one or two vehicles at a time; the make, size or even condition of these purchases was often of little relevance, the main importance being the prize of the Carriers Licence attached to it, especially if it was an Open 'A' with the words 'Goods - Anywhere' attached as a condition.

Some of the vehicles bought in this way were four furniture vans, three from Jimmy Williamson and one from a Mr. Shanklin. The Pratts from Brampton were to eventually sell their two ERF four wheeler flats to Stan although the two Pratt brothers continued to drive these vehicles for their new owner. But the biggest take-over during the wartime period were the seven vehicles of Fred Laidlaw as Robsons bought themselves a large chunk of the exacting business of milk collection.

Transporting milk is, and always has been, a job that has to be done seven days a week, 52 weeks a year. Rain or shine, cows do not switch off production merely because it is a weekend, and although the milk traffic can be particularly tying, it is a job which means guaranteed use of the vehicle and so regular pay.

Cumberland wasn't any different from the rest of rural England and servicing the numerous dairy farmers were many haulage concerns who specialised in milk transport. Although there were some isolated movements in bulk by road tanker, the vast majority of cartage was done using churns to the dairy and then by bottles out of the dairy after the milk had been processed.

Many owner drivers were involved in this traffic although Fred Laidlaw was one haulier whose fleet had grown to seven strong, mainly on the back of milk haulage. Six Bedfords and one Commer were what he was running in 1940, all these being petrol engined four wheelers. Base was the rather grand sounding New Hall Garage at Gilsland, which sits right on the Northumberland/Cumberland border in the valley of the River Irthing.

Having such a relatively large fleet, Laidlaw also had a big catchment area of farmers to serve although the milk collected was generally hauled east, down the South Tyne valley to the dairies at Stocksfield, Gateshead or Newcastle. Stocksfield is particularly remembered for its size of milk churns and whilst most dairies tended to use those of 12 or 15 gallon capacity, Stocksfield used a smaller 10 gallon size but also real back breakers at 17 gallons.

The pattern of the Laidlaw churn carriers was almost like clockwork. Starting off with a load of empty churns, the driver did the daily round of farms on his list. Normally placed on large roadside stands, the loaded milk churns were transhipped to the back of the vehicle and in their place the driver would leave the same number of empties for the next day's

'Border Patrol is another well used Robson name although this Foden DG was second-hand when bought into fleet about 1946 from the North East's Tyneside. The DG was the standard long distance Robsons vehicle of the era and sported heavy steering, heavy clutch, but the luxury of an openable windscreen.

GR 2596 was Bedford chassis number 141341 and first registered on 2nd March 1936. Regular early driver of the vehicle was known as 'Blind Alfie' because of the fact that he wore dark glasses all the time. Although it was used for removals, one of its main jobs was to ferry consign-ments of fruit and vegetables from Thursby into the Carlisle markets for the respective market gardener stall holders. The vehicle had an unladen weight of 2ton 9cwt. 3qtrs. 14lbs. and passed on to BRS but was scrapped in 1950.

'Border Envoy' is another ex Thistle Albion which had Herbert Bell as its regular driver. The vehicle dates from 29th September 1938 and at 10 years old still looks well. The vehicle is loaded with cartons of Hadrian Paint being run from Haltwistle to Darwen in Lancashire.

cargo of milk. Once fully loaded with full churns, the vehicle was set for the run across country to the dairy. Into here the loaded churns were lifted off, emptied into the storage vats, then were quickly washed prior to being put back onto the lorry as the empties for the next day.

Generally speaking these milk carriers were never without churns on their back — either empty or loaded - but in view of the relatively long distance that the Laidlaw vehicles ran across to the North East, a novel trick was used to improve utilisation. Rather than load the empty churns back onto their respective vehicles, Fred sent a large cattle carrying vehicle to the dairy that could carry three loads of empty churns stacked up inside it. Whilst this vehicle made its way back to base at Gilsland, the empty churn carriers would run into the mills of Tyneside to collect back loads of animal feed to be delivered back to the farms in Cumberland.

Laidlaw thought long and hard about improving the efficiency of his churn carrying vehicles. He even bought two old buses which he stripped of the passenger carrying compartment and replaced with a longer than usual platform body, but these weren't a great success. George Jackson well remembers these old girls, a scar on his lip ensuring that he will never forget. Being a strapping 16 year old driver's mate, George naturally had to swing the handle to get the vehicle started. But with the dog engagement at the end of the starting handle suddenly coming loose, George catapulted his face into the ground at a terrific rate of knots to cause the self inflicted injuries.

Laidlaw engaged mates like George to help the drivers lift the 'Stocksfield Killers' — the 17 gallon churns — but once Fred had sold his fleet out to Stan about 1943, getting rid of the mates was the first saving the new owners made as they told the drivers they would now have to load on their own. "But I'm seventeen, Mr. Robson", George Jackson fibbed to Stan, "I can drive one of the Bedfords." He certainly could drive as George 'Willy' Richardson had taught him how whilst on their rounds, so, with drivers being in short supply, George talked himself into a driving job that he kept for nearly two years before being called up into the Armed Services.

Once the sale to Robsons had been completed, it was decided to incorporate all the ex-Laidlaw vehicles into a new company under the name of Border Hauliers (Gilsland) Ltd. Operations continued out of the old tin shed that was New Hall Garage. Based at Haltwistle were the vehicles of another Robson company, that of the Hadrian Transport Co Ltd which had its registered office at Garden Terrace, although the vehicles were kept behind the Conservative Club in Sun Yard.

Back at Carlisle the end of the war prompted the Robson/O'Reilly combination to adopt a new trading title of Robsons Hauliers (Carlisle) Ltd. This was to reinforce the Carlisle reference to the company, a reflection now that Robsons of Carlisle were going country wide, and they didn't want their fine fleet being confused with any other similar haulage names of Robson.

Border Transport (Brampton) Ltd was another Robson concern and had a fine sound to its title although like the similar grand sounding Hadrian Transport, this concern only had a fleet size of two vehicles.

When it came to additional comforts for a vehicle, Stan Robson was rarely very enthusiastic. 'Border Ensign' sports a fog lamp and a lockable tool box, these being extras which would have been added on by the vehicle's own driver. The Albion is ex Thistle Transport being registered on 26th November 1937.

'Border Beacon' was an example of the 127 model which was first introduced by Albion in 1935. This vehicle dates from early 1937 and although only rated for about 4-5 ton of payload, both Thistle and Robsons got far more fee earning cargo on it during its 11 years of service.

On the face of it the growing Robson empire was an administrative nightmare, but the creation of so many smaller concerns was a deliberate ploy prompted by the eagle eye of accountant O'Reilly. The tax laws then in force were apparently worded so that each particular limited company had its own fixed margin of profit before tax began to be calculated, so, as the Robsons vehicles were spread quite legitimately round at least four different concerns, they were liable for far less tax than if they had been all bracketed into the one individual limited company.

The various assessments of tax wasn't the main thing affecting post war road transport, it was the political thinking prompted by a change to a Labour Government in the 1945 General Election. They soon made it clear as part of this Socialist mandate that rail and road transport should come under Government ownership. The rail network may have been large but at least it was a network set up round a fixed structure of railways and perhaps was amenable to being totally nationalised.

Road transport, however, was entirely different, and covered everything from delivering your daily pinta to moving a 100 ton transformer. How all this could be efficiently managed without the flair, imagination and downright competition of a free transport structure was the main argument that the Road Haulage Association and other like minded organisations began to voice most strongly.

Noel O'Reilly put his all into supporting the case against nationalisation of road haulage, and toured the north west of England to argue his point. He reckons his greatest claim to fame is how he shared the bill boards at Rochdale Town Hall with Gracie Fields. These announced that he was to speak in support of a free transport network, while Gracie was to appear the following night letting her singing voice give a slice of musical entertainment that was highly popular at the time.

To say that many hauliers got jittery at this time was perhaps an under statement. Alexander Smart used this period to seriously look at the viability of Thistle Transport, and sensed that in all the circumstances, it might just be right to sell out that far flung offshoot of theirs as a going concern. Whilst not being blinkered to what may be just over the horizon, Stan Robson had stronger nerves than some. But the sheer awesomeness of buying out the Thistle Transport concern on 4th February 1947, is put into perspective, when you learn that in acquiring those vehicles, the Robsons fleet doubled in size overnight.

Thistle ran an assorted fleet of multi wheelers, wagon and drags, furniture vans and even flats on milk churn work. With Thistle covering a wide spectrum of haulage, the blend with Robsons own operations was ideal, and although the trading name of Thistle Transport was naturally retained for tax reasons, the vehicles were quickly repainted into the two tone red of Robsons and adorned with a strong sounding 'Border' name. It's not surprising that the Royalty chain soon got exhausted although in 'Empress', 'Duchess' and 'Emperor' there were some fine titles, their evocative vision being only beaten perhaps by the picture created with the name 'Border Supreme'. Albert Robson however will tell you that in many respects this vehicle was supreme to very little.

During the summer months a surge from the milk producing cows meant Robsons were asked at times to move this excess across to the North East. Whilst a demountable tank was ideal for this intermittent traffic, few of the drivers liked the job. With no baffles in the two compartment tank, the surging liquid meant for a very uneasy ride. 'Border Emblem' was a petrol engined Albion and new to Thistle Transport in 1936. Regular driver was Bobby Platt who lived in a caravan parked in the old Thistle yard.

The streamlined Hornsby paint job sets off the ex Thistle 'Border Legion' very well. When destined for an early finish, the Robson milk drivers found themselves working as 2nd or 3rd men on an afternoon's removal job. Such was the questionable quality of some of the houses visited on this work that the milk men called this type of job 'the bug run'!

Albert had travelled down to Sandbach to collect the new Foden eight wheeler and its first sight should have indicated that the vehicle was never going to be quite right. Instead of being the normal bright two tone Robson red, Albert recalls that the Foden paint job was a rather odd red and orange.

But going onto the road on 2nd July 1947 it was to be its performance that was its most disappointing feature. True the revered Gardner 6LW was never going to be an exceptional performer in producing first 102 bhp and then rated up to 112 bhp which equated to just over 5 bhp per gross ton of the fully loaded vehicle. But Albert reckoned what should have been his pride and joy was close to being an embarrassment. Trips back first to the engine maker at Patricroft and then to Sandbach met with little success. Gardner simply fitted a flow meter to the engine pump and when this checked out as normal they couldn't come up with any reasoning as to its lack of gut stumping power.

Albert had been given 'Border Supreme' after coming back to Carlisle after six years in the Army, it being the Services that had also interrupted George Jackson's time at Robsons. He had asked Stan for a job back on the milk wagons, but with no vacancies then, he was pleased to take the offer of a new Foden four wheeler 'Border Renown', which took to the road on 5th March 1948.

George can well remember his first trip, which was to take a load of shoes from the Bata factory at Maryport down to their factory at Tilbury. Bata is well recalled, for they even arranged accommodation for the Robson long distance men inside the Tilbury premises. Unloading here it was then an empty run across to Pershore to pick up a load of plums to be delivered back in Maryport at Lakeland Foods.

Powered by the four cylinder Gardner engine, the little Foden never missed a beat, although getting a top whack of 35-40 mph was a bit of a struggle, as George remembers driving with his left foot pressing firmly down on top of his right foot, which in turn was hard down on the acclerator pedal.

This haul, like many others, started off on a Sunday, hardly ever a day of rest for the true long distance men. It took some doing at times but most men managed to get home for a Friday whilst Saturday morning was usually spent on maintenance of your vehicle, provided you were loaded up to leave home again on the Sunday morning once more.

The tramping long distance men of old were virtually a legion to themselves. In some ways they had a totally isolated job, yet in other respects the camaraderie of other trampers meant they had friends all over the country. The Robson men had a fair degree of autonomy from that distant Carlisle office and naturally each had their own little black book full of telephone numbers for back load contacts or overnight accommodation no matter where their Gardner powered Fodens took them. If you couldn't get a load from anywhere else there was always Bibbys at Liverpool as a last resort, that would source some Cumberland bound traffic.

The trampers were men who had to enjoy this form of wanderlust although it rarely fitted in to what could be described as a traditional domestic life. The loved ones they left behind had to have strong wills as well as perhaps a good

memory to remember who their husbands were. Perhaps the lack of time spent at home is best illustrated in remarks chalked on the driver's noticeboard by one disgruntled wife. "Question — Mam, is my Dad dead? Answer — No son, he just works for Robsons."

George Jackson stuck at the tramping life with 'Border Renown' for over a year. But the overtures to get a job with him at home more often became incessant, and with a vacancy being created on the milk work, George was transferred across to one of the three milk churn wagons that were being run out of Carlisle. Just like the ex Laidlaw fleet which had been left on its own to slowly expand at the Haltwistle depot, the ex Thistle milk wagons had been hived off to form the company of Border Deliveries Ltd. They still worked out of the same Durranhill base, although with the purchase of Thistle Transport, Stan had moved across to the bigger premises just across the road.

The old base had been a compact staging post for a small fleet, but it was starting to burst at the seams with the influx of more vehicles. The garage is remembered for its hand operated fuel pump, a loading stand where goods could be transhipped and an awkward slope to the floor that caught out one visiting driver. With handbrakes not being totally reliable in days of old, he had been standing in front of his vehicle as it slowly rolled down the slope of the garage floor and pinned him — injury free — up against the sturdy garage wall.

The vehicles running the milk out of Carlisle tended to be old Albions; this type of chassis being liked because of their longer body length than the Foden and also their lower

(Above left) *Supreme by name and supreme by presence, it was only its road going performance which let down this fine looking DG eight wheeler CHH 385 was first on the road on 2nd July 1947, Albert Robson being given regular custody as driver to this vehicle. Having the 6LW engine — virtually the standard power pack of the day — this Foden never seemed to have the same gut pulling power that the Gardner engines were renowned for.*

(Above right) *Befitting of its size, BHH 516 was named 'Border Majestic' after it joined the Robson fleet as part of the Thistle Transport acquisition. First registered on 3rd January 1944, its regular crew at Thistle of driver Bobby Bell and mate Geordie Gibb stayed on the vehicle when it came to Robsons. Its load, seen here, is the rubber material that Wellington boots are made from, en route from BATA's factory at Tilbury to their other factory at Maryport. Such was the size and speed of this vehicle that it could only achieve one round trip per week between Cumberland and Essex albeit running loaded in both directions.*

loading height onto that body. Starting off originally with an Albion built 4 cylinder petrol engine, when these power packs were worn out Stan shoe horned the 4LK Gardner engine into the chassis in their place. It may take some believing but these 4LK engines were reportedly getting 26 m.p.g. and that was running at 10-12 tons gross on the four wheelers.

The Foden-Gardner combination had done Stan proud, in fact, when asked about his hopes for the future by a Foden publication in 1946 he went on record to say "I aim to make my fleet 100% Foden. It takes something to stand up to the hills and roads of the Fell country of Cumberland and Westmorland and that is what my Fodens have done. They look

Although a sister vehicle to 'Airman', the Willy Douglas vehicle of 'Border Clarion' was recalled as having performance as dead as a bat. Both Albions dated from July 1940 when they started life with Thistle Transport. It is recalled that 'Clarion' got stopped by the police as suspected of being overloaded when climbing Alconbury Hill. It wasn't its load of empty tin cans that made it go so slow but just its general lack of go.

good and are good. I must mention the magnificent service which Foden have given especially through the difficult war years. They have never once let me down and it has always been a smiling service."

It's probably only natural that the Foden representative would be keen to repeat Stan's glowing remarks about his marque of vehicle. However the same article related what Stan termed to be the reasons behind their success in "Service, hard work, foresight and fair dealing with customer and workman." But to the historian it was probably the last remarks in the article which were to have the most significance. "We are all ready, if we are only allowed, to get on with the job, despite it's uncertain future."

The uncertainty of that 1946 observation came to a head on the 27th July 1949. It had been over a year since the Nationalisation Act had first started to eat its way into the heart of the free transport network, but that summer day finally saw the end of Robsons Haulage (Carlisle) Ltd when it and it's sister companies were acquired by the Labour Government.

The records of the Road Transport Executive — later renamed Road Haulage Executive — which operated under the British Transport Commission give cold details of the acquisitions. Forming part of British Road Services, North West Division, Carlisle Group — Head Office being at 83 Lowther Street, Carlisle — the companies were bought as units, with C179 Thistle Transport (10 vehicles); C180 Robsons Haulage (36 vehicles); C181 Border Transport Brampton (2 vehicles); C182 Hadrian Transport (4 vehicles).

True, Border Hauliers (Gilsland) Ltd and Border

'Border Laird' sports a new paint job mocking its ten years of previous hard life with Thistle Transport. It is carrying an old railway box that Robsons delivered in great numbers throughout Cumberland. Whilst the best were utilised as secure stores, others were used as horse boxes and so required unloading in some strange locations. Depositing them was normally down to strong arms and strong pushing legs.

Deliveries Ltd — the milk wagons — weren't touched as their rather low key local operations weren't deemed to form part of the big nationalisation plan, but in essence Stan Robson's life was close to being finished. What had been months and months of agonising over had finally happened, but even then he couldn't relax. "I'd better hang on, just in case they want to know something about the business," Stan told Kitty as she implored him to get away on holiday, but the phone never rang, as Stan just sat and waited.

August 1949 was a confusing time for the driving staff, for overnight most of them were transferred onto the BRS books, although the Carlisle milk men had literally to take to the streets as their old depot was now now longer open to them, as it too, had been compulsorily acquired. But it seemed to be Stan who suffered the most. Never a man who enjoyed the best of health, if ever any of his vehicles was having mechanical problems he used to lie awake for hours trying to work out the difficulty. It was obvious that the trauma of this situation would take its toll as his fitness declined dramatically and he was rushed into hospital with life apparently just oozing out of him.

TB (tuberculosis) was eventually diagnosed, and as Stan just seemed to be fading away N. T. O'Reilly realised things had to be done and they had to be done quickly. N.T. found out that Switzerland was the closest source of the best American penicillin and with no more ado he charted a De Havilland Rapide from Air Navigation and Trading Co Ltd of Blackpool. Capable of carrying up to eight passengers, the plane was fitted with twin Gypsy Six engines which gave it a

'Ranger' gleams in the daylight, if lacking its number plate of AHH 999. Pride of place on the grille is the commercial version of the Automobile Association badge. All Robsons vehicles were in the AA and drivers were issued with a standard box key. This membership continued until the AA suddenly rocketed their prices and the link to Robsons was thus broken.

Whilst many of the old petrol engined Albions were to have Gardner diesels fitted as replacements, 'Viking' is recalled as having a Perkins four cylinder diesel fitted instead. Quite a fly machine, it still proved a difficult starter from cold. Regular driver Freddie Howes had to use an ignited rag pushed into the air intake to encourage ignition. HH 9753 was an ex Thistle vehicle dating from 26th November 1937.

George Douglas had been at Robsons for a couple of years before he received this ex Thistle Albion in 1947. George draws attention to the design of the container which reveals a specially made downward step underslung to the rear of the platform body. Once the tailboard was dropped on its chains, the effect of this step allowed for an easier progress into the van body, whilst handballing loads inside.

range of about 600 miles and seemed ideal for the urgent medical journey across Europe to Geneva, rushing Stan to some of the best medical aid.

Taking off from Kingstown, Carlisle, the plane had to stop at Lymm in Kent for customs clearance before going on to Paris to refuel. But too much time was lost here and by the time the Canadian Pilot 'Woody' was climbing over the Alps, the cold November night meant icing on the wing grew to be too much for the frail aircraft. Obliged to turn round, the catch 22 situation was that there wasn't enough fuel to get back to Paris and sure enough, about 70 miles short, one of the engines cut out as it ran dry. Hardly more than 5 or 10 minutes flying was left in the other engine so 'Woody' had to come down. On the first two descents all the landing light picked out was a forest of trees, but on the third descent an open field was greeted like the promised land. Showing the highest degree of professional skill Woody made it down onto the ground, although the passengers recalled that perhaps in hindsight they were pleased they couldn't see what Woody had to do.

Whilst Woody soothed his nerves on a cigarette and Nurse Audrey Cunlin comforted the stretchered Stan, N.T. and the second man of the aircrew - nicknamed Flying Officer Kite - went out for help. They were to discover later that they were near the village of Fere-Champenoise, with the nearest large town being Sezanne. But their goal that night across the muddy fields was a single light shining in the distance, a farmhouse that was to provide help and refreshments, plus fortunately a big Peugeot estate car that could accommodate the full length of the stretcher.

By car back to Paris, Stan finished the journey to Switzerland by train but having had the luck of the Gods with him to weather such a traumatic flying experience, it was obvious that a disease like TB wasn't going to get the better of him. Aided by the best of medical help, the following May saw him recover enough to make the return journey back to Carlisle, but this time by the somewhat slower method of car.

Home was to be 'Wrayside', a large house on the Wetherall side of Carlisle that Stan was to enjoy for the next 36 years. Originally having just paddocks at the front and rear, as adjacent fields became available for sale, Stan bought them up and was to develop a farm that eventually grew to 140 acres. What started out really as a form of therapy grew to be almost a second business, yet still in a relaxing form, as Stan put his life back together. With his road transport fleet being decimated from around the 70 mark down to just over double figures, relatively little of Stan's time was needed in this domain, for the milk wagons seemed to run to their own particular day-in day-out timetable.

Whilst Lance Keen ran the east Cumberland vehicles out of the Haltwistle depot, Gladys and Tommy Robson looked after things at Carlisle. However, all the milk men tended to have a rather independent life as George Jackson recalls that the garage for his four wheeler was a piece of grass verge not far from his home. The wagon was strategically parked at the top of a hill so once the parking mechanism had been withdrawn — a large stone was that chocked under the back wheels — free wheeling downhill meant the engine could be

The Reo Speedwagon certainly lived up to its name for ability to cover the ground and 'Border Clipper' as its name reflects this pace and grace. The Reo dates from 12th October 1939 and was new to Thistle Transport Ltd. Regular driver was Robert 'Bud' Parker, whose main attribute was in his ability to find his way round London to a multitude of backwater unloading points far quicker than anyone else.

fired into life without resorting to that huge starting handle that poked itself forward out through the radiator.

At this time George ran 'Border Duke' — a maturing Albion four wheeler Reg No. HH 9172 — that had actually started life with John Laing & Son Ltd on 25th February 1937. George had a list of 20 farms for daily collection, all of which were in the Walton area, this being north east of Carlisle. Also running churns out of Carlisle was Joe Bell, who also had a petrol engined Albion — the ex Thistle Transport 'Border Lassie' — and Ellis Bell, who had a small ERF four wheeler 'Border Roamer'. Ellis had actually come to Stan on the promise of a half a day's casual driving work but was to stay on in a permanent fashion for 42 years. Naturally with a pedigree like that Ellis became to be accepted as the expert on milk although all the three Carlisle churn wagons had their own different itinerary of farms to cover. Running into the local Border Dairy in Carlisle meant an early finish to the driving day, although as the farm at Wrayside began to expand, there was always plenty of work to do there to finish the shift off.

The only days they took advantage of that early finish and not work up at Wrayside was perhaps Saturday and Sunday, for unlike the general haulage men, the milk drivers worked every day of the week with 7 a.m. being the normal morning start. Getting a holiday was a bit of a joke and the only way you could get a full weekend off was if the other drivers would work a double run. This meant either collecting two sets of churns or perhaps doing deliveries of bottled milk to the dairies down the coast at Silloth, Maryport, Workington, Distington then across to Keswick.

Working the regular double shift meant even less time at home on a weekend than normal. To get round this George Jackson recalled that as a Sunday treat his wife Bet would go down to Carlisle by bus with his daughter Shirley. They would arrange to meet George in the Albion and in order to see more of each other they would spend the afternoon together on deliveries. Shirley would go into a basket mounted on the top of the engine cover, although one day it was a matter of necessity that Bet came with him. George became stricken with the milkman's nightmare — an awful bad back — and it was only with her help that he could transfer the loaded churns back across on to the Albion.

It was to be the milk wagons that kept the heart of Robsons transport alive. True, they only worked a beat across the northern farmlands but in 1951 the fickleness of politics saw a Conservative Government elected into power in place of Labour. Their mandate clearly stood for the de-nationalisation of long distance road transport which in essence would mean the end of the BRS monopoly. The winds of change were set to blow yet again as the fire of free enterprise was fanned into life.

Many miles from Westminster Stan Robson drove his tractor round his Wrayside farm and he smelt the breeze. His thoughts wandered back to happier days with his huge 'Border' fleet, as he considered his options. The telephone had never stopped ringing as his customers of old began urging him back into transport. The trauma of 1949 had nearly cost him his life and the first reaction was that he didn't want to get back into that heartache again — or did he?

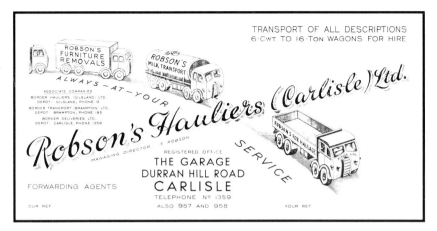

The pre-nationalisation letter head displays a fine attribute of art work and of course, a mention for a famous Border name.

ROBSON'S FURNITURE REMOVALS

ROBSON'S MILK TRANSPORT

ALWAYS – AT – YOUR – SERVICE

Robson's Hauliers (Carlisle) Ltd.

MANAGING DIRECTOR S. ROBSON

ROBSON'S FOR HAULAGE

TRANSPORT OF ALL DESCRIPTIONS
6-Cwt. TO 16-Ton WAGONS FOR HIRE

ASSOCIATE COMPANIES
BORDER HAULIERS (GILSLAND) LTD
DEPOT GILSLAND, PHONE 12
BORDER TRANSPORT (BRAMPTON) LTD.
DEPOT BRAMPTON, PHONE 195
BORDER DELIVERIES LTD.
DEPOT CARLISLE, PHONE 1359

REGISTERED OFFICE
THE GARAGE
DURRAN HILL ROAD
CARLISLE
TELEPHONE No 1359
ALSO 957 AND 958

FORWARDING AGENTS

OUR REF   YOUR REF

(Below) A few of the press cuttings relating to Robsons' activities during the latter part of the 1940s.

July 30th/49

"double Summer Time" from April 13 to August 10.

MILK GOT THROUGH

Tanker Took Supply from Carlisle to Newcastle

Carlisle Milk Distributors, Ltd., rendered a very valuable service by maintaining their milk supplies in Carlisle and district 100 per cent. during the severe weather. The producers, who supply milk to the Border Dairy, who in turn supply Milk Distributors, Ltd., in spite of the treacherous road conditions, managed to get a high proportion of their milk into the depot at Shaddongate, Carlisle. The Border Dairy was able to get a tanker of milk through to Newcastle by road, and thus kept vital supplies going.

The tanker was provided by Robsons Hauliers, Carlisle, and was driven by Adam Steven, who performed a remarkable feat. Every day of the blizzard, except Thursday, he managed to take his vehicle through from Carlisle to Newcastle, and thus kept vital milk supplies going. He would have got through on Thursday also but for the fact that the road was blocked by a string of motor cars near Gilsland.

LETTER TO EDITOR

Haulage firm nationalised

SIR,—I feel certain that very few of your readers will be aware that on Tuesday last at midnight the first compulsory acquisition under the Road Transport Act of 1947 in the Carlisle district took place. Previous acts of nationalisation have rather tended to seem far removed from personal contact, involving large coal mining companies and large public utilities which are of an impersonal make-up.

In the case to which I refer, namely Robson's, Hauliers (Carlisle), Ltd., the matter is brought right to one's doorstep as the business concerned is that of a fellow citizen and is very much a monument to the individual hard work and business ability of Mr Stan Robson, whose wide experience of road transport matters extends over twenty-five years.

Even the courtesy and helpfulness of the officials, whose task it was to carry out the acquisition, does not compensate for the fact that one's head goes to rest at night the owner of a fine thriving concern, only to awake in the morning minus the result of a life-time's work.

This is the first compulsory acquisition. Others will follow, may be it will be the grocer, or the tailor or the ironmonger next, who knows?—Yours, etc.,

N. T. O'REILLY, Hon. Sec.,
Carlisle Sub-Area, Road Haulage Association, Ltd.

Aug 2nd 1949

HAULAGE

Nationalisation of local firm

SIR,—On Tuesday last, the first haulage firm in Carlisle was taken over (compulsory acquisition), and so has ended the firm of Robson's Hauliers (Carlisle) Ltd. Over 25 years Mr Stanley Robson has worked long and hard, giving a fair deal to his workers, keeping his vehicles in first-class condition and giving the public a service second to none. Mr Robson is only one of thousands who have been, or will be, swallowed by the Socialist machine—nationalisation.

Many Socialists in our city think it right and proper that this haulage firm should be acquired by compulsion. What do they care for the risk Mr Robson took when he put everything he had into his first vehicle? What is it to them that he is now in poor health due to the efforts he has made to keep his firm running when he should have taken a rest, only to have it taken away by the action of the men put into power by Socialist votes?

Instead of being of any help to Carlisle, this acquisition will prove a loss in local revenue to which Robson's Hauliers were no small contributors. Other firms will follow, individual efforts through hard up-hill times will be rubbed out, and by the same doctrine we went to war against in 1939.—Yours, etc.,

DISGUSTED.

Albion

'REIVER'

MODEL FT.107K

LIGHT 6 WHEELED CHASSIS WITH 4 CYLINDER OIL ENGINE

ALBION MOTORS LTD., SCOTSTOUN, GLASGOW, W.4

Although Robsons hadn't got back into using as many Albions as they had before being nationalised, the Company was still famous enough for Albion wishing to use them on the front of this 1955 brochure.

CHAPTER THREE

A century not out

Whilst the Government may have been changed overnight on the whim of the electorate, the laws of the land took slightly longer to re-arrange. But the prospect of de-nationalisation gave many butterflies in the stomach in heady anticipation. To men like Stan Robson it was a period of time more like gazing through a shop window to see what was going to be on special offer — provided you could wait.

Truthfully many haulage people — Robsons included — had never come completely out of transport. Not just in ex-empted traffics like the milk churn work, but also by reading the fine print of what the nationalised legislators did allow for. One such loophole was the 'C' hiring licences that could be issued where a haulier's vehicle could be run on a dedicated user basis, the only restriction being was that the dedicated user had to pay the wages for the driver of that vehicle.

But when N. T. O'Reilly read the fine print of the regulations he found that one vehicle could in fact be interchanged amongst several 'C' hiring licences and Robsons did in fact utilise this loophole with two of their Gilsland based Fodens.

The settlement of Haltwistle, about five miles from Gilsland, may seem in a strange place in the South Tyne valley, sort of midway between Carlisle and Newcastle, but its secluded location was positively endearing to many especially during the war time years. It had developed into quite a self contained town with its three big transport requiring concerns, those being Oliver & Snowdon — Agricultural Merchants, Kilfrost — makers of de-icing fluid, and Smith & Walton, who were famous for their paints. Although BRS did in fact have a depot in Haltwistle — situated in the railway station yard — Robsons weren't afraid to compete against them, as best they could, bearing in mind their relative monopoly.

Smith & Walton ran a fleet of their own vehicles on paint distribution, their motto being "Hadrian Paints are good, Centurion Paints are better", but there were occasional deliveries that just had to be made on a contractor's vehicle. The reason behind this was that Smith & Walton did make some specialised products that were in fact sold on, under other manufacturers' names. Robson driver Dessy Bright can recall one regular trip down to Merseyside, where as soon as the loaded drums of Smith & Walton's were rolled off his vehicle, a chap stood ready with a stencil set, to immediately re-brand the drums as having been made by the recipient.

It thus didn't seem right for one of Smith & Walton's own vehicles to deliver into a situation like this, although on the rare occasion when they had to, the distinctive Smith livery was covered up by brown paper and sticky tape before it entered the receiver's factory.

No such problem of livery concealing for the Robson vehicle which was allowed to carry its load south under its 'C' hiring licence, issued for Smith & Walton's goods. However, once the vehicle was unloaded, a telephone call back to O'Reilly in Carlisle — who arranged for the insurance of the vehicle to be changed — then allowed the driver to remove the Smith & Walton 'C' hiring licence disc from his windscreen and put up an Oliver & Snowdon disc in its place. It was then quite legal to go round to the cattle cake mills in Liverpool and

'Border Marquis' was one of about half a dozen S18 Foden eight wheelers that were bought during late 1955 from a sale at Warrington. This Roger Kenney photograph taken in Old Hall Street, Liverpool recalls the fact that Robsons were more than just occasional visitors to that part of North West England.

(Right) Seen duelling with a load of pallets in the premises of Metal Box at Carlisle, 'Cavalier' was another of the second hand Fodens bought at a sale in Warrington. A load of pallets like this should have meant for a quick journey time with little weight involved, but the wind resistance created dragged you back to a normally fully loaded pace.

load up with a cargo of animal feed as a back load to Haltwistle. Once back at base the next load may have been out of Kilfrost and all it took was yet another telephone call to re-arrange the insurance to make things legal, after, of course, interchanging that small windscreen disc.

Albeit totally above board, this 'musical chairs' procedure with licence discs was rather administratively complicated but it did keep the Robson toe dipped into the waters of general haulage. But now the tide seemed set to change and the figure of George Flenley enters the Robson story and the combination of Robson, O'Reilly and Flenley wasn't far from making one massive impression in the world of transport.

During 1952 George Flenley was Traffic Superintendent for the Carlisle Group of British Road Services. His upbringing however, had been totally free enterprise dominated, for in joining the heavy haulier Edward Box Ltd in Liverpool as a management trainee in the late 1930s, his experience was set to vastly broaden as Box became engrossed in a large group of transport concerns known under the short if rather apt name of Hauliers Ltd. Initially the set-up was an amalgamation between Box's and the Tunstall based small haulier of Beresford, Caddy and Pemberton Ltd but fairly quickly other concerns spread country-wide were absorbed into this group. It thus proved an ideal experience for the growing Flenley, but not surprisingly the solidly based Hauliers Ltd was an early casualty of the nationalisation compulsory purchase programme.

In the following shake up George took the promotion offered, which meant him travelling north, but this wasn't in

any way an easy option. Together with the ex Highes & Beattie depot at Carleton, the Carlisle Group also encompassed the old Johnsons of Gilcrux depot at Aspatria, the ex Henry Bowman depot at Bigrigg near Egremont, the old Cumberland Roadways depot near Workington as well as two smaller sub-depots at Cockermouth and Penrith. But it was its geographical location on the main England — Scotland A6 route that made Carlisle so busy as almost nearly all of the British Road Services fleet had reason to call on this ideal staging post at one time or another.

But hardly had George got into his stride with BRS when Labour were voted out of office and rumours about what would happen to the BRS empire began flying thick and fast. The main worry was that everything would be de-nationalised overnight so it's not surprising that drivers, traffic clerks and even traffic superintendents began to consider their options.

In a tightly knit transport community like Carlisle both Stan Robson and George Flenley were well aware of each other's reputation. Whilst Stan had always said that he had no intention of going back full scale into general haulage, the prospect of buying 'just a few' grew to become too big a temptation. With Stan already being quite busy at the thriving 'Wrayside', George was asked if he would manage the new operation and on 1st February 1953, what was to become Robsons Border Transport Ltd staked its place in the transport arena. The newly acquired fleet, bought straight from an early BRS sale in Manchester, were all four wheelers, they being five Jensens and a sole Bedford.

Base for this new fledgeling concern was in Metcalfe

Resurrecting the old 'Warrior' name was rather fitting for this Guy Otter which went into service on 24th April 1950. It was registered to Border Deliveries Ltd at 34, Lowther Street, Carlisle, which was the office of Noel O'Reilly's accountancy business. Although seen loaded with churns, regular driver Adam Stevens tended to work the vehicle on bottled milk delivery down the coast of West Cumberland.

17th September 1951 was when 'Border Princess' was first registered to the company of Border Deliveries (Gilsland) Ltd. Seen loaded with bagged flour, Robsons hauled a lot of this traffic from Carrs Mills at Silloth to the bread bakers on the North East coast. The Foden's sister vehicle 'Prince' had a strange demise when it caught fire on the top of Shap.

'Border Raider' was given new to Albert Robson when it came into service on 16th February 1954, it being registered to Border Deliveries Ltd. Close examination of the door decal reveals the name Robsons Border Transport, but not the letters 'Ltd'. This indicates that the concern was using R.B.T. as a trading title before it was fully incorporated. The sister vehicle to 'Raider' was 'Border Patrol' coining the remark when the vehicles ran together, "Oh look, the Patrol is chasing the Raider".

Street, Carlisle, in a garage that had previously belonged to another Carlisle haulier, J. W. Watts. Given a corner in this garage to work out of was the tyre fitting business of Jack Blacklock. Whilst he was obviously allowed to make sure Robson's rubber was kept in order, a concession to him sharing the garage was that he had to let the Robson's drivers ring in for instructions on his telephone, which meant that the single Robson's telephone line could be kept open to allow for possible customers calls.

Metcalfe Street also meant that the itinerant milk wagons at Carlisle had somewhere legitimate to call home, as prior to this base being bought they had tended to live either at the dairy or on the grass verges close to their respective driver's homes. Even the registered office of Border Deliveries Ltd had been at 34, Lowther Street, Carlisle, which was the business offices of Accountant O'Reilly.

The milk wagons at Gilsland were also given a new home at Mill Bridge Garage at the thriving metropolis of Haltwistle, although day to day management of these vehicles stayed in the South Tyne valley with Lance Keen. All the Robsons vehicles were to share a new paint scheme, the two-tone red of old, even with its gold lettering, was far too close to the colours of British Road Services vehicles, which continued to dominate the roads of the land. Maroon and cream was to be the distinctive change that was adopted, all the fleet being painted by the expert craftsman, Jimmy Hornsby. A man who could use a paint brush like anyone else used a pen or pencil, Jimmy also shared this expertise by teaching his art at the Carlisle Technical College. He was still a man who

(Above) *Whilst the cargo going onto the back of 'Border King' is obviously ammunition boxes, in the middle 1950s this type of small container was ten a penny. They were still ideal for all sorts of heavy traffic like assorted scrap or surplus, even if handballing such a small concentrated weight was difficult. Dickie Newall is the long serving Robsons driver seen on the left of shot in glasses.*

(Right) *Robsons' first static lifting device consisted of a set of three legs in the Durranhill yard, so this ex builders crane was a big improvement. However, being hand operated it was still nerve wracking to operate, especially if you tried to slew the jib in high winds. HHH 25 is 'Border Victor' and was new to fleet in December 1954.*

Whilst the Chinese Six Foden set Stan away with the marque way back in 1937, 'Border Duchess' was a rare copy of that configuration to come to Carlisle. Harry Millican got his 1954 Christmas present five days early when he was given this vehicle new. Sporting the Foden two stroke engine, it had a lower geared back axle which made it a far better vehicle to drive than the high geared flying machines of 'Raider' and 'Patrol'.

lacked confidence in himself and naturally some of the drivers tended to rib him by suggesting that newly painted names might be out of alignment as 'it didn't look right'. Jimmy would take such a suggestion very seriously indeed, although one matter he wouldn't stand for was anyone decrying his favoured Carlisle United football team; voices were regularly raised if anyone took the liberty of insulting their prowess.

With a change in the laws relating to income tax, it meant the end of the need to have so many small limited companies, so all of the Robsons vehicles were eventually to run under the banner of Robsons Border Transport, which in essence, was a compilation of all those names of old. One O'Reilly devised concern, however, that was kept going entirely separately, was Ullswater Finance Ltd based at Penrith. If Robsons Border Transport were to borrow money from anyone to finance expansion, they may as well borrow it from some-one in the family and O'Reilly ensured the interest rates they offered were far better than the normal H.P. rate.

It was to be capital, or the ability to lay hands on it, which was to be the key in building up a haulage business in the early 1950s. For not only did you have to buy your vehicles, the most important thing was to buy the carriers licences that allowed you to operate them. True, you could always apply to the Traffic Commissioners for a licence, but with so many BRS vehicles being up for sale — along with their Special 'A' licences — getting a carriers licence for free was a non starter.

The BRS fleet was gradually being run down with their vehicles being sold off in varying sized lots right up until about 1956 when the general practice ceased. To buy them

The size, the design and just the sheer presence of the new company offices proudly proclaimed that Robsons Border Transport Ltd had at last arrived. Whilst George Flenley's Hillman stands in the centre and next to Stan's Bentley, the main mode of transport for the boss in latter years was a regularly changed new Rolls Royce with the perpetuating registration of SR 999.

you just had to submit the highest tender, a procedure termed by some as a blind auction. One North East entrepreneur remembered from this time, was noted in how he would tender successfully for huge lots of up to 50 vehicles a time. He would then sell them off individually with a new certificate of weight, as a carrier's licence for a vehicle was linked to the respective vehicle's unladen weight. However, not being satisfied with the vehicle's true unladen weight, this man reportedly added ballast weight to the under-side of the body before the check weigh was carried out. With a heavier unladen weight ticket, it was an accepted practice to be able to charge higher prices for these vehicles/licences to the queue of prospective customers. This procedure may be difficult to comprehend in this day and age where it is lightness that is the premium, but the rather poignant part to the story is that the weighbridge he always used for the check weighs was situated at the Blind School in Newcastle.

Stan Robson had to accept the tendering procedure to acquire the ex BRS vehicles, even though it stuck in the gullet when he realised how little he had been paid for his premium fleet when he had been literally forced to sell up less than four years earlier. Paying out say £500 meant you hardly got much more than a load of scrap on wheels but Robson vowed that if that was what he had to pay, then he would certainly get his money's worth of work from the vehicle out of the deal.

In buying Jensens, Stan bought a vehicle that due to its high use of aluminium in its build was probably worth more when it was scrapped than what he had paid for it. The vehicles were recalled as being ideal for 6 ton loads, but put say

6¼ tons on them and they would start to sag in the middle. However what George Flenley found them ideal for, in having a long 24ft. platform body, was that they were capable of carrying almost as much cargo as a big eight wheeler, provided that cargo was one of empty tin cans.

Working for the Metal Box Co in Carlisle was one of the first sources of regular traffic for the newly formed Border fleet. True, this was only on a sub-contract basis to start with as rather ironically it was the Clearing House set-up of Thistle Transport that had the main contract to organise most of the Metal Box's traffic movements.

Clearing houses have always been a strange facet of the road haulage scene as many of these concerns don't even have any vehicles of their own. But in simply being a middle man between customer and a haulier, the clearing house was allowed to take off a regular percentage in the rate paid for the job. The ironical part to Thistle being involved in taking its percentage cut was that this aspect of the old Alexander Smart business was not a slice that had either been bought out by Robsons nor had it been absorbed into BRS during the nationalisation programme.

With so much emphasis on cash, both in income being shaved by clearing houses and expenditure being enlarged to pay for carriers licences, what suffered was the life of the driver, as the quality of the tool of the trade — his lorry — varied in the extreme. Whilst noise, rattles, draughts and the sheer lack of any comfort whatsoever was of regular concern, it was the extreme cold during that worst six months of the year that took its toll on the driver's health. Albert Robson

Specification sheet 1 — JAH 800

		Type: FE. 4/14	Standard or Tipper:	Works No.:	

BORDER TRANSPORT
...SIDE
...ETHERAL,
CARLISLE

Type: FE. 4/14
Length of Body: STD.
C.C.
Standard or Tipper:
Works No.: 40418

Cross Member (Rear):	Gen. Arr.	REMARKS
3999	FEA. 3999.	Frame:- Fuel flitch plates, flex members FE4038. FE4039. 1off. FE4002 2off. FE4003 2off. FE4004 2off. FE4005 2off. FE4006 2off. Elect. equip:- fuel electric change speed - Cab heater & demister

Fuel Pump No. HW 139.	Engine Suspension Unit EB15A.	Engine Controls: Unit EC18A.	Fuel Supply Pump Make	Dynamo: 24 V/t Type LS22A No. 111990.
Radiator: Make Heavy duty] Type R8F	Starting Gear: Unit ESG5D.	Change Speed Gear: Unit C316G.	Gearbox: 2A/2 de Geater Type GB38H No. of Speeds 8	
Clutch Type: C10E Foot Pedals: Unit CBP16 A	Decompressor: Unit	REMARKS Radiator:- Complete FE3649. - Spec faw cowl FE36	
Rear Axle: Unit RA44A Carrying mad FG8063. Make	Rear Wheels: Type 6.00x20 Dunlop heavy duty] Offset 5.625.	Rear Tyres: Michelin Section 10.00x20 Make	Tyre Carrier: Disc type 8 tube Carries FG3445 Make
Front Axle: Unit FA29E. Make	Front Wheels: Type 6.00x20 Dunlop heavy duty] Offset 5.625.	Front Tyres: Michelin Section 10.00x20 Make	Brakes (Front): Type Unit BL40A.
Steering Arms 1st Axle 2nd Axle	Fan: See eng. Type	Service Tank: Unit FT20D. Type 32Gal.	Bogie Shaft: Make Unit
Diff. Housing: Type No.	Worm or Bevel: Ratio 7.00/6.25 Type WG22P WG22J Make	Spring Shackles:	Tipping Gear: Make

Mudguards:- Front M26A. Rear not req.
Engcovers:- BD25A.
Pulling jaw:- Front FE3674. Rear S6076 Rigid Patt.
Bumper Bar:- BB4A. supplied loose. Bonk to fitted
Thermometer:- FG6956.

Type. Cab S18Uee front
Body. Not Req.

16'-1"

The specification sheet of 'Border Roamer' illustrates the details on the Foden vehicle and obviously the fact that the Mark 2 version of the two stroke was just being released.

Specification sheet 2 — KHH 466

CUSTOMER:—
ROBSONS BORDER TPT.
DURRANHILL ROAD,
CARLISLE.

Type: FE. 4/14
Length of Body: C. C.
Standard or Tipper:
Works No.: 40416

Frame: Length: 25' 4 3/4" Section: 6"	Cross Member (Rear):	Gen. Arr. FEA 4009	REMARKS
Engine: FD 4 Unit Make: Foden No. MK2/3701	Fuel Pump No. DX 212 Make	Engine Suspension Unit EB15A.	Engine Controls: Unit EC24A	Fuel Supply Pump Make	Dynamo: 24 V Type LS30C No. 113205 Make S
Speedo. Cable Length 13'0"	Radiator: Make R20A Type	Starting Gear: Unit ESG5B.	Change Speed Gear: Type GB38H No. of Speeds 8	Gearbox: twin shp Starter: 24 V Type LS30C No. 63236. Make S
Exhaust Pipe & Silencer: fuel shpttk cranking device Unit S40A	Clutch Type: C.10.G. Foot Pedals: Unit CBP14E	Decompressor: Unit	REMARKS Rad. will be Cooled. FE 4164.
Rear Springs: Make No. Unit RS38C	Rear Axle: Unit 8A54A Make	Rear Wheels: Type 6.00x20 Offset 5.625"	Rear Tyres: Michelin Section 10x20 Make	Tyre Carrier: Incl air Lyne & tube Unit SWC34B	Brakes (rear): Type HB24H Unit BL49A
Front Springs: Make No. Unit PS45A	Front Axle: Unit FA29E Make	Front Wheels: Type 6.00x20 Offset 5.625"	Front Tyres: Michelin Section 10x20 Make	Brakes (Front): Type Unit	Cardan Shaft: Type PS23 H Flanges 70 "/16"
Steering Gear: Type Unit SG 159	Steering Arms 1st Axle 2nd Axle	Fan: see Engine Type	Service Tank: Unit FT 21D Type 50 Gall	Bogie Shaft: Make Unit	Intermediate Shaft: Unit LS20C Drg. No. 5' 4"
Steering Drag Link: Unit DL14C.	Diff. Housing: Type	Worm or Bevel: Ratio 7.5:1 Type WG 20P. Make Browns	Spring Shackles:	Tipping Gear: Make	Tip Pump: Unit Make

REMARKS Cab heated & demisted HD .1A. Bumper Bar 6A
Mudguards Ft M. 42A.   Special thermometer 1-96956
Engine cover. BD 30A.
Pulling jaw Ft FE 4130.
" " Rear S6076 Rigid.

Brake Rods:

Cab Type. S20 CAB 13A.
Body.

Wheelbase 16' 1"

DATE SUPPLIED.
24 – 1 – 1957

This Foden spec' sheet has a misspelt registration, it being applicable to 'Border Patriot' which was registered KHH 446.

recalled that many drivers tried using a bed of straw in the bottom of the cab to try and combat the cold. The reasoning behind this was that straw was used quite widely in stables with animals, and they always seemed to be able to keep warm enough. Whilst the straw might cut down on draughts from around the pedal holes, the only one time that it really created heat was if the driver would accidentally drop a lighted cigarette into the straw and the whole pile would catch fire!

George Flenley recalled a different ploy to heat generation that he was told about when he was riding shot-gun in one of the old Box vehicles in a period of his management training which saw him dispatched to experience the pointy end of transport. The cold was incredible, George recalled, but when he asked the driver how he managed to work in such an extreme of temperature, the driver demonstrated the strangest of solutions. What he did was to take his shoes and socks off and then drive with bare feet for about half an hour. Obviously his feet then became colder still, but when he did put his shoes and socks back on, the relative warmth in doing that made him feel much more comfortable.

It's thus not surprising that drivers weren't too happy about getting some indifferent vehicles, although one Robson driver of old was known to complain about anything and everything. His vehicle, his load, his pay, or even the weather always prompted the same dour reply in that of "I'm sick." It's not surprising that this particular moaner was nicknamed "Willie Sick". But for Willie and all the other drivers, new vehicles were eventually arriving into the Border fleet, with of course, the older hand-me-downs being used on milk traffic.

It was good business sense to put the older four wheelers down to Haltwistle in the twilight of their career as although the work was seven days a week stuff, it wasn't as demanding as running up and down the country on general haulage work. What was demanding was in getting some of these old vehicles started, for some like Dessy Bright's old ex Fire Service Albion, was definitely an 'Armstrong' vehicle. Converted to have a Gardner 4LW engine, the morning start was normally a case of assistance from three men on the rope attached to the starting handle. Once the engine had warmed through use of a decompression lever, Dessy could swing the engine on his own before the little lever was moved back to allow the engine to compress itself into action.

At close to 20 years old the little Albion had some strange idiosyncrasies. It's huge glazed cab was more like a greenhouse in the summer, whilst the right hand mounted gated gear shift had an awful habit of seizing itself in gear. The only way round that dilemma was to climb out onto the back of the body, move some of the churns out of the way, then by lifting up a trap door, access to the gearbox was gained by loosening off a screwed down plate. Once the innards were exposed it was an easy matter to free the seized mechanism.

This apart, the Gardner powered Albion rarely missed a beat although it met with the strangest of demises. Dessy was loading churns from a stand on the side of the famous Military road — the old Roman road which runs parallel to the main A69 cross-country route. An almighty crash coming from the front of the Albion drew Dessy's attention to the fact that something had gone wrong. On walking round he found

'(Left) *Swift*, *Victor*, *Revenge*, *Reliant* *Rebel*, *Linnet* and one unknown are lined up left to right with respective drivers Bobby Mawson, Jimmy Bury, John Robson — who was Stan's nephew — and mechanic Tommy Bowman. At the time these four cylinder Ford Thames four wheelers were liked by both drivers and management alike.

(Left) *Befitting the fleet number 100, this Foden two stroke S20 eight legger was named 'Border Century' when going new into service on 2nd January 1957. Geoff Young was the vehicle's normal driver although he isn't the figure in the Roger Kenney photograph. The bagged cargo is out of Tate & Lyle's, Robsons hauling a lot of this traffic from Liverpool up to storage in Greenock.*

a car implanted head on into the grille and driver's side of the Albion. The female driver — who only suffered a small cut in writing off the two vehicles — complained of steering failure as to the cause of the accident. She was more upset that her samples as a representative in selling Ladies underwear were now blowing round the countryside in all directions.

As a replacement to the Albion, Dessy received from Carlisle an ex Army ERF recalled for its strange pre-select mechanism to its fifth gear. Once the gear lever and clutch had been used to start away from rest and build up the speed in the normal way to fourth or 'top', fifth gear or overdrive top was obtained by pushing the lever forward — without pressing on the clutch — and then when required, dipping the clutch would engage the highest ratio.

The ERF was quite a premium vehicle to be sent down to Haltwistle as this joined a mixed collection of Albions, Dodges — also with five speed gearboxes, Morris Commercials, Austin Loadstars and the two well remembered Bristols. 'Border Rover' and 'Border Raider' were the respective mounts of Billy Bell and George 'little' Trotter. Converted buses, they were recalled as having smart cabs, 24ft. long platform bodies and single line unassisted hydraulic brakes with only questionable stopping power. Whilst the Bristols may have been all right whilst pottering round on the milk, it was when they were occasionally wandering farther afield that they weren't so predictable.

Robsons were asked to move a large number of battle tank engines, which weren't excessively heavy, albeit rather bulky when packed in transportable form. The vehicles were

thus normally loaded with an extra case stacked double deck form on the top which meant for a load far higher than the normal churns. In running across country, Boroughbridge was a regular overnight stop, the Robson men tending to stop in the town at The Anchor, rather than at the popular Kelly's Cafe on the southern outskirts. George Trotter decided he would try and be first to the digs one night but couldn't understand why the rest of the Robson convoy took a different route into Boroughbridge. All too late he saw the wooden footbridge over the road and even with his footbrake fully applied, plus the huge handbrake ratcheted on, the poor stopping power of the Bristol showed its true colours. The rather flimsy foot-bridge didn't stand a chance against the strongly packed tank engines and it was sent flying from its mountings. Fortunately the bridge wasn't in use at the time and whilst George learnt a salient lesson to his driving technique, the incident also underlined the need for more powerful air braked vehicles.

But the days of the Bristols were numbered as new vehicles started to come aplenty. Not necessarily all new from the makers, but new to Robsons, they included a batch of six Scam-mell 'Rigid Eight' eight wheeled flats. Starting out life well back with Youngs Express, they had passed through BRS own-ership before coming north to Carlisle. Old fashioned, even ungainly looking, the Scammells did at least have the favoured Gardner 6LW engine and air brakes on most of their eight wheels. What did arrive new, and in numbers, were Ford Thames four wheelers with snub little bonnets concealing first petrol and then four cylinder diesel engines. Not really amongst the heavyweights for load capacity, they were re-

Robsons very quickly realised that warehousing was to be a major key in any advancement in the transport business. John Slatty is seen topping up from store his Thames Trader 'Border Winner' which came into service on 24th July 1957. John was a native of Scotland who moved to Penrith when Scottish based hauliers required change-over drivers to be located in this part of Cumberland.

JSM 262 was a maturing ten year old Chieftain when George Jackson got it for his milk round but his new 'Border Yeoman' was still a big improvement to his old ex Thistle petrol engined Albion. Seen with son Alan on the Crosby road, milk drivers will note the ecstasy of lightweight aluminium cans being carried on the low slung body.

called as being quite brisk across the ground with a top speed of 50mph.

With the deluge of vehicles into the Border fleet the premises at Metcalfe Street quickly became unsuitable. However, the search for somewhere better soon made it obvious that the way Robsons were expanding then, it would have to be a place built from scratch on a green field site.

Whilst Stan had regularly demonstrated a Midas touch to almost anything he became involved in, the buying of the land on what is still the Carlisle base of operations, didn't exactly go to plan. Stan's foresight knew that something exciting for the area was being planned, and in buying a large piece of land on the south side of town he felt quite pleased with himself. Situated geographically just to the east of the established Durranhill Road, the area was destined to be called the Harroby Trading Estate (later renamed as the Durranhill Estate). But the local Council were anything but pleased with Robsons' actions and set about obtaining a compulsory purchase order to buy the land off Stan. The only way Stan could steal the slightest possible march on the Council over the affair was to sell a plot of this land on, before the compulsory purchase limitations took effect.

The fortunate recipient of this bit of land was good friend Bobby Hind who ran a business of bodywork building which naturally had long encompassed fitting up all the newly purchased Robsons vehicles. Rather strangely this was the only plot on the whole estate that wasn't compulsorily bought by the Council back off Hind. All the other occupants of the new estate had to rent the land, although the one concession

the Council did give to Stan was that Robsons were given the pick of the Estate for their newly planned H.Q.

By 1956 Robsons Border Transport Ltd had taken up occupation of what was one of the finest examples of a haulage contractor's base. Well planned office accommodation, workshops and stores. Whilst it wasn't intended that the growing fleet would be at base very much, over 13,000 sq.ft. was set aside for vehicle parking. Perhaps of even more significance was the 15,000 sq.ft. of warehousing to cater for goods in transit, the Robson 'nouse' for good business sense identifying that it was to be this particular avenue that would prove to be of vital importance to any haulier worth his salt.

Delivering those goods in transit Stan favoured unashamedly the Foden. His words of 1946 in how he proclaimed his faith in the Sandbach marque were still very much of relevance ten years later. Whilst fleet numbering may be of little significance because the way older vehicles drop out of operational use, the day that number 100 came up for display was something rather special. Naturally it had to be a Foden — one of the latest S20 eight wheeled rigids — that was to be registered KHH 395, whilst in choosing 'Border Century' as it's name there was to be little in the way of argument.

If anything 'Border Century' merely signalled that Robsons Border Transport had come of age and become a transport force to be reckoned with. Whilst growing very quickly may be a capability of many, keeping themselves firmly established at the top of their field for the next 25 years was going to be more difficult later. The key to this factor was in how to achieve operational success.

(Right) *Bonded traffic like this palleted load of Scotch Lager was not something that Robsons was licensed to store, so fork lift driver Gordon Mallison is seen simply transhipping onto another vehicle. 'Border Queen' was new on 23rd December 1957 whilst 'Border Supreme', seen in the rear, came into service on 13th April 1959. The clock on the warehouse wall is surrounded by the expression 'Robsons — always on time'.*

(Below) *The Scammell Rigid Eight 8-wheelers were bought in the mid 1950s as a means of quickly expanding with strong, licensed load carriers. 'Border Patrol' like the other Scammells, had only a single drive rear bogie which was recalled as giving the vehicle poor traction ability, especially when running light. Not a lot of weight on 'Border Consul', the six wheeled Thames Trader, seen carrying a load of empty tin cans.*

(Above) *Stan Robson is seen in conversation with driver Johnnie Little. Stan — much to wife Kitty's annoyance — would hardly wander far without his cap. 'Border Dandy' came into service on 3rd January 1962, and became destined to be chopped into a four wheel tractive unit. It ended up on the Durham moors near Tow Law before being saved for preservation by Robert Chicken.*

(Right) *Even the most diminutive of vehicles received a name, this Joe Donaldson photograph illustrating one of the company's smallest. 'Valet' is a name still in current use, PHH 919 dating from 25th April 1960. The Ford Thames 7cwt. van being a fitter's runabout.*

CHAPTER FOUR

Serving
the
customer

By 1958 Robsons Border Transport were able to count the size of their fleet into three figures, it being their rather unique structure of management that created a platform both for growth and stability. Whilst Stan Robson was always going to be the boss, he had reached a position in his life which was almost luxurious. It was now a time when he could indulge in formulating and instituting an expansionist programme and also be able to supervise the engineering side of the Border fleet. Being a born mechanic, it was probably in this latter area that he found so much satisfaction.

Ensuring that the accountancy side of the business was kept in order, Noel O'Reilly's target for success was not merely in the growing number of cream and maroon wagons, but it was aiming for the first time that Robsons were to achieve £300,000 in annual profit. Even thinking of those sort of figures indicated that things had changed a lot over the last 20 years, for in those early pre-war days, management meetings were normally held every Monday night at 21, Burlington Place.

It was on a Monday that Stan and Kitty normally treated themselves to a night out at the pictures in Carlisle. Going round to the O'Reilly house after the movies for a bite of supper, Stan and N.T. then went through the figures to see how they would be able to pay the drivers' wages on the following Friday.

The twenty year turn round had encompassed the headache of nationalisation but it also reflected the contribution of George Flenley to the Company, George being given an open brief for traffic matters and in the day to day dealings with the growing number of Robsons customers. Taking up some shares in the newly created Company meant that both O'Reilly and Flenley had a vested interest in the success of Robsons although this didn't prevent an element of friendly rivalry as to the relevant pecking order of these two aspects of the business.

N.T. naturally made it perfectly clear that it was the accountants who ran the business. In disagreeing George Flenley summed it up by saying that it was the operational people, like him, who made history — accountants simply wrote about it.

In fairness it is probably the operations of any haulage fleet, in the first instance, that this class of service business is all about. Although in contributing to the Robsons formulae George Flenley had looked closely at what the competitors in general and British Road Services in particular were able to offer.

Not the total monopoly they were at the start of the 1950s, BRS were still the biggest carrier in the land although it was to be this huge size that meant sometimes they let themselves down in the standard of service they could offer their customer, with Kilfrost at Haltwistle being a case in point.

This firm of industrial chemists had originated from the Home Counties, they being actually bombed out of London during the Second World War. Firmly re-established in Northumberland, the destination of a large amount of their de-icing fluid was the Northolt airfield near Uxbridge in

Whilst Robsons certainly worked their vehicles hard, many of the Fodens were strong enough to withstand this treatment and still be ready for more when it came time to move on to their next owners. The Roger Kenney photograph (left) *shows the Gardner powered 'Unicorn' in Liverpool, whilst* (right) *Michael Cook pictures it in showground service at Penrith, 15 years on from when it first came into service in 1960.*

Middlesex. Even during the strict period of nationalisation they had made some use of the pair of 'C' hiring Fodens of Robsons, but in the main they had tended, like many others, to use BRS as their main haulier. Never any complaints in southbound deliveries of their fully loaded drums of chemicals, but what was exasperating was in not getting back their empties.

Although BRS had a small depot in Haltwistle — which was to close about 1956 — the long distance men bound for Northumberland tended to end up either in Newcastle or Gateshead, quite some distance away across in the North East. The empty Kilfrost drums were dropped in the yard until the traffic office remembered about them at a time when they had an empty vehicle that happened to be Haltwistle bound.

The times that these two situations coincided were few and far between with the result that the Kilfrost production set-up became stretched. They could of course, have bought more drums but this would have been inefficient capital expenditure with those empties lying about in distant BRS depots. So, when Robsons became established in a size to be a viable alternative to the Government concern, Kilfrost swapped their haulier with one of the main requirements from the Robson men being to bring home the empties. Driver Dessy Bright recalled that each drum was worth 10/- (50p) a time to the haulier and vehicles regularly managed to squeeze 80 empties on board in one go. A rather lucrative back load to Northumberland for a customer well appreciating excellent service, it did, however, require a sympathetic

driving technique for such a high, light load over the long 300 mile haul.

The reasoning behind Robsons getting this foot-hold into Kilfrost was in being able to offer a service that the customer ideally wanted. The BRS organisation seemed unbeatable in theory with having such a vast national network, but at times there could be great inter-depot rivalry — sometimes occasionally stretching to bloody mindedness — whereby the level of service to the individual customer may marginally suffer. It was vowed that this form of malaise wouldn't infiltrate into Robsons, so the decision was made that everything would be run from Carlisle — the self contained milk operation at Haltwistle apart.

Such a strategy seemed to go completely against the grain for in the early 1960s almost every other haulier the size of Robsons, ran his vehicles via a chain of depots spread round the country. It was almost a status symbol to have your vehicle's livery plastered with as many different depot addresses and telephone numbers as possible. Robsons, in comparison, seemed almost quaint in having only that sole Carlisle base, but this fact underlined one cause of efficiency.

The reasoning behind the Robson philosophy was simple. No matter how small a depot you had, you still had to pay rent and rates for it. The depot would have to have a manager, perhaps an assistant for him, a traffic clerk, a secretary and probably a telephonist. The manager would doubtless need a company car and as the size of overheads continued to grow it became apparent how much Robsons

When naming Albion vehicles Stan always made a preference for Scottish sounding titles, although the one adorning his first LAD cabbed Reiver did lack a bit of imagination. Fleet number 184 was new on 21st June 1960 and like all the Albion stable mates offered both long body length in a light nimble vehicle.

were saving — when compared to their competitors — by simply not setting up a chain of far away staging posts.

But what these other hauliers got out of their chain of depots was an ample supply of return traffic, although, even running solely from Carlisle, Robsons extensive national operations was quoted as averaging out with only 10% being empty running. True, the Robson telephone bill indicated that it was this form of communication which linked office and drivers together, but it was to be a chain of agents throughout the country that was the main source of back loads.

Many of these agents were hauliers in their own right, the relationship to Robsons being one that was established through a long period of time in contact with each other. One such agent recalled from this period was that of Silver Roadways, which at the time was the transport arm of the Tate & Lyle Sugars Group, a concern which Robsons worked a great deal for. The contacts that George Flenley had made through his time both at Edward Box and in BRS days were also utilised, although the arrangements with all these agent/hauliers were ones that were reciprocated and loads furnished from the Carlisle area for their vehicles if and when required.

The chain of agents established a Robson network around the country and it also proved an ideal framework to support the next extension of service which was based on a tried and tested BRS formula. It wasn't an idea that BRS had dreamt up but their enhancement to the concept of collect your goods today, trunk them overnight from one end of the country to the other, then have them delivered to your

Coming into service on 13th December 1960, 'Border Viceroy' sports its Hind built triple dropside body which was a type of construction that was never really liked by many of their respective drivers. Although the S20 was the Robson fleet backbone at this time and gave sterling service, having a front, breakdown, towing jaw was of almost standard Robson specification to this marque of vehicle.

(Left) *When seen brand new, the Thames Trader looks a fine transport machine. The long wheelbase platform dropside was used for its first year on the testing overnight trunk work before going onto roaming. When finally pensioned off onto local work, the milk men thought their heaters were tremendous. SHH 282 is 'Border Pennant' and also came into service on 13th December 1960.*

(Left) *With shining bright metal and resplendent livery, the S20 Foden was a fine ambassador for Robsons. Roger Kenney pictures the wandering 'Border Roamer' in Liverpool not long after it came into service on 20th February 1961. The office of Silver Roadways was a usual haunt of the Robson driver when in this town in search of an outward bound load for his vehicle.*

customer first thing tomorrow, was a level of service that many were trying to emulate. Double shifting your vehicle — using it both during the day and night — meant for far better efficiency in cutting down on under used resources. It did mean however, that three different drivers would have to be used on the vehicle and one of them at least could not be based at Carlisle.

Robsons staff were employed as far afield as Glasgow and Stoke-on-Trent. Shunters were also based at Warrington and Preston, still without any form of Robson owned base in these towns. All were linked to Carlisle by the reliable medium of the telephone, although it was the organisation created at Biggleswade that ensured Robsons had a firm centre of operations in the South East of England.

The arrangements created here saw about fifteen men eventually employed at Biggleswade, eight on days and seven on nights, the smooth running of what was created being reflected in how it stayed in being until after Robsons were bought out by United Glass in 1980. With all the staff receiving their orders by direct link to Carlisle there was once again no need for any form of depot here, although the Robson men did adopt Bells Brook as their unofficial base of operations.

What was an old stretch of the A1 road that had been made redundant and blanked off when the new Biggleswade by-pass was built, proved to be an ideal change over point for the trunkers. Although two night men did run non stop from Carlisle, the Biggleswade night men tended to work a change over system whereby they swapped vehicles with southbound Carlisle men so that all of them would end up at

home at the end of their shift. Two different change over points were used, Knutsford in Cheshire and Micklefield in West Yorkshire. The latter one on the A1 was opted for if the load was destined for interchanging yet again at another agent's depot in the North East.

With Biggleswade being only about 40 miles north of London, the Capital was the natural final destination of most of the southbound traffic that was shunted on by the daymen. The catchment area they could be asked to cover, however, was still fairly extensive with traffic being destined for places as far apart as Peterborough, Kings Lynn, Colchester or even Southampton. The Carlisle office would normally pass details the night before of the pre-arranged back loads which had to be picked up and brought back to Biggleswade in time for the night men setting off north.

Fuelling for the vehicles was done via an arrangement with Sandy Filling Station, a few miles further north up the A1. Long before the arrangements of nation-wide bunkering agencies were created, Robsons had set up their own system where fuel in bulk was delivered into the tanks at Sandy. For a small administration fee the garage kept a check of what the Robsons vehicles used up and once stocks got low, Carlisle was notified and a fresh top-up was arranged.

In theory what was a straight forward system was only kept running smoothly by the dedicated staff involved. With vehicle breakdowns being a trunk operation nightmare, liaison with local garages meant that Robsons were given a very high priority should any repairs be required. The Robson reputation of high standing had filtered this far south and as

It became regular practice during loading that sheets were thrown onto the top of the vehicle cab but continued abuse like this first made the roof buckle and then the skin would actually split. The small wooden roof rack cut down on this flexing and became a standard fitment on most of the rigid flats. 'Phantom' dates from 24th February 1961.

Robsons high standing in the transport field made them a natural choice when a customer needed the best of service with delicate traffic. The Gardner powered 'Monarch' like the rest of this quartet is carrying special carbon blocks made in the North East of England and hauled across to Chapelcross. These blocks were closely machined before being transport on again to Sellafield.

one garage man remarked, "When we saw a Robson wagon at the door we would drop everything to get it back on the road. We knew for definite it was a job we would be paid for."

It was only natural that the Foden flagships were first choice for the demanding night trunk traffic. Stan continued buying regularly both eight wheelers and then artics from the Sandbach factory. His dream of old that he would like to become 100% Foden never came to fruition as the fleet list of 1964 shows an almost even split between heavyweight Fodens and lightweight Fords.

Following those early brand new Ford Thames 'Costcutter' four wheelers, Robsons invested heavily in the Thames Traders — rigids and artics. The Trader was recalled as being ideal, for it could be looked after on a one driver — one vehicle basis, but on a needs be requirement the Traders were used on the night trunks to Biggleswade. Not really built to withstand the phenomenal mileages involved, after a year of this they were given less testing work and eventually — to many of the milk men's delight — sent to Haltwistle. Even now Dessy Bright can still recall the delight of wallowing in the warmth from the Trader's heater — luxury at last.

Not really reckoned for its excessive heat generation, the Gardner engine remained the Robsons favourite for Foden fitment throughout the '60s. However, relenting to overtures from the Foden directors, some Fodens had come to Carlisle in the 1950s with engines of an entirely different nature and two specific ones with an entirely different cab.

Foden weren't the only makers of the two stroke engine in this era, as the Commer TS3 was produced in far

greater numbers, albeit for use in vehicles at lighter weights. Produced either as a four or six cylinder version, the Foden 'stroker' was also used for static generating, in marine use and one particular four cylinder engine was reportedly fitted into a Mercedes sports car. Only done for experimental purposes, the car was still apparently capable of reaching 100mph.

It was to be this high level of performance, especially when compared to the leisurely Gardner, that was the big attraction of the two stroke. Continually being developed, the final six pot versions were made to produce well in excess of 200 bhp at a time when Gardner were only capable of 112 bhp from the 6LW and 150 bhp from the 6LX. Far lighter in its unladen weight than a conventional four stroke engine, the drawbacks to the sweet sounding two stroke — apart from a question mark over reliability — was in requiring both a multi-speed transmission linked to it and a far different driving technique to get the best from it.

Unlike the Gardner that seemed to have an endless amount of pulling power no matter how slowly it 'revved', the two stroke had to be kept turning at a very high speed to keep producing the goods. Fodens built their own 12 speed gearbox, the differing ratios engaged by use of two different levers. The first versions of these 12 speeders required the left hand to shift both the levers, although subsequent improvements saw the three speed range change lever moved across to the dashboard and mounted so that the right hand fingers could do the work.

Getting the 12 speeder, especially mated to a stroker, work as Foden had designed was a work of art and many a

UHH 188 is 'Border Chief', the Thames Trader tractor which dates from 6th November 1961 being coupled to a York semi-trailer. Its load is a mixture of empty tin cans together with some heavier tin ends. A lot of this traffic went to an animal feed manufacturer at Barrhead, recalled for its very high standard of cleanliness.

Whilst the dropside body wasn't overliked by the drivers, it was a terrific boon if the cargo being carried was offal. This was like trying to carry bags of jelly and so couldn't be roped and sheeted in the conventional way. Robsons carried a lot of this traffic to Liverpool and Sheffield, loads that were always deemed to be urgent. 'Meteor' was new to Robsons on 23rd January 1962.

driver could be driven close to frustration. A slightly easier transmission to comprehend was fitted to 'Border Patrol' and 'Border Raider' which saw the main gearbox augmented by a two speed splitter which was worked by a small lever mounted on the steering column. The respective drivers of these two Fodens — Geoff Young and Albert Robson — tended to drive with the left hand on the main gear lever with the index finger of the right hand resting on the electronic 'trigger'. Timing the gear shifts on the two stroke had to be done at exactly the right time.

'Patrol' and 'Raider' were also recalled for their Bowyer built cabs, the type of which was taken up by many brewery purchased Fodens, as the cab allowed seating for a three man crew. The doors on this type of cab were particularly strange as they were hinged at the rear (to open at the front) rather than the other way round as with a conventional cab door.

The one main concern to drivers with this design was that if the door was accidentally opened whilst the vehicle was on the move, the rush of passing air would tend to whip the door open wide, rather than try to push it shut. With the windows only opening to a half way position, the space created didn't allow for a driver to lean out when he was reversing, so, all in all, these two vehicles weren't everyone's favourites.

To many transport enthusiasts the Foden two stroke was a sound they would never forget, but to Stan Robson it was a sound that he had mixed feelings over. There were quite a few 'strokers' in the fleet at this time, but like highly strung stallions, they could be temperamental. Developing your trunk services was only done on the back of reliable vehicles.

True there was the occasional breakdown, but this prompted the traffic office to search round for a roamer that may be close to hand. Juggling this vehicle into the trunk system meant the roamer's driver had to sit and wait for the broken down vehicle to be repaired. The trunkers could move a lot of traffic over a lot of miles, but like a chain, once a link was removed then it came to an abrupt halt.

The Robson night men were both the highest respected and highest paid of the driving staff, but not every Robson driver wanted their sort of life.

Bobby Mawson was one man who worked the Robson wagons from 1940 until he retired in 1982. True, there had been a brief interlude with BRS as overnight in 1949 his month old Foden had been compulsorily acquired. Like most of the Robson drivers Bobby had been almost forced to stay with his wagon and go over to BRS, there simply wasn't any other alternative employment. Even more misery when the new Foden was taken off Bobby and sent to Manchester, with a weathered Vulcan being left in its place. It was at least soon to get new tyres, for on its first trip with Bobby it suffered four blow outs.

Once settled on BRS Bobby was given a van bodied four wheeler and a line of work which he stayed on for more than 25 years. Bobby even kept the job when he went back working for Robsons in 1954 and although it was virtually the same run, week in — week out, Bobby enjoyed the life. Every Sunday Bobby's Ford would leave Carlisle destined for London and the South Coast. Inside the van would be up to 40 different deliveries of cloth from Ferguson Printers (Carlisle)

(Above) *The backdrop of Tower Bridge, London, shows 'Warden' in a typical Peter Davies' photograph, his efforts during the 1950s and 60s ensuring a fine historical record of goods vehicles used in those days. Whilst the day shunters may have used this bridge simply as a way of getting to and from Biggleswade, the roaming drivers recalled that they used a plentiful supply of good digs on the other side of the river. 'Warden' came into service on 5th March 1962.*

(Right) *Recalled for always wearing a beret, George Jackson was one of the long serving milk drivers who worked this type of traffic out of Carlisle for about 20 years. OAO 427 is George's second 'Yeoman' which came to Robsons during September 1962. The Chieftain has chassis number 73746K and was new to John Bowman of Dalston on 2nd July 1954.*

(Below) *Whilst weight was never a problem in hauling these loads of new empty drums out of Lancashire, getting the most on board — height limits allowing — was only made possible by the use of some specially designed racking that cradled the top layers of drums safely in position. 'Rebel', which dates from 11th March 1963, is coupled to a Loadleader semi-trailer.*

Robsons were to use both the Albion 4 cylinder powered Chieftain as well as the Leyland 'Super 6' version. 'Border Provost' was one of the former types and was new into service on 25th April 1962. The vehicle, which is seen on tramping work, was to end its days on milk work, first with George Jackson, and then with current employee Andy Carruthers as its driver.

(Below) *A rather puzzling pair of vehicles in Robsons livery were the two Commers, run on a sub contract basis by Ronnie Yates. Called 'Jenette', this rigid had been extended by means of a York trailing axle. 'Diane' was to be affixed to Commer artic EHH 99C although both names were later transferred onto Volvo F86 artics that were painted black. The six wheeler is pictured on the A1 at Blyth outside the Hill Top Cafe.*

Ltd, who are perhaps better known under the brand name of Viyella. Back loaded with anything suitable, Bobby hardly had time to deliver this before reloading with yet another 40 drops of cloth. Saturday morning was, of course, spent on maintenance of the vehicle, ready to leave again on the Sunday.

Bobby and his different Fords hardly missed a beat for just on a quarter of a century on this same run, but on 18th May 1978, the passing of time dictated that Bobby should, perhaps come off the road, so he went into the Carlisle warehouse to work. Perhaps reading from the unsolicited testimonial given to Bobby by Fergusons at the time he finished driving gives some indication of the thoughts they had of the Robson service. "Please accept this small gift in appreciation of the valuable services you have rendered to this Company. We appreciate that at many times you have acted beyond the requirements of your normal duty, and in doing so have managed to create much goodwill amongst our customers. We knew that goods consigned through you would always, whatever the weather, arrive safely. With grateful thanks."

More than 50 years after first starting with Robsons, the vehicles Bobby drove are still vivid recollections, and it is their names that first come to mind — 'Princess', 'Swift', 'Swallow' and 'Bronco' were all Mawson mounts and in a fleet that would touch 180 strong, it is this individual Border name that made so much difference.

Stan was fairly philosophical about the reasoning behind the naming of the fleet. He was quoted as saying the names had a certain publicity value, it furthered public

Making regular use of the same sub-contractors was a Robson adage. George Flenley contended that such use could always be mentioned when applications were being made for extra vehicles on your 'A' licence as it showed you had work for extra vehicles. The Roger Kenney photograph is of a Guy Warrior belong to long serving subbie Percy Hunsworth.

Not only having a distinctive shape, BEV 937B was also recalled for its rather distinctive colour, as it was painted all red. As the name 'Trialist' suggests it was a demonstrator vehicle which was destined not to catch on. It was used on the London trunk and regular driver Geoff Young recalled the Cummins powered Ford could really fly.

relations and it imbued each driver with a pride in his own vehicle. What Stan wasn't quoted in saying was something that anyone who knew him was aware of, and that he had a personal feeling for all of his vehicles, and giving them individual Border names was something which he derived great personal satisfaction from.

It had never been a Robson aim to keep on growing but once the snowball of excellent service had started to roll, then it just picked up extra traffic as it went along, thus increasing the need for more vehicles. Better utilisation of the fleet was found by going headlong into articulation and by 1965, examination of the fleet list shows that it is new tractive units that are arriving in droves. The days of classic Foden S20 eight wheelers like 'Border Empress' Reg. No. LHH 770 were numbered as Foden tractor units like 'Border Countess' Reg. No. AHH 594B were taking over the mantle of the fleet flagship.

This wasn't to be the end for S20 eight leggers like 'Empress', for with a reputation of being well maintained, the sold-on vehicles were snapped up by people like Gwynne Bowen's of South Wales for yet more hard work. Many were passed on to showmen's duties whilst one S20 was chopped down into an artic tractor.

By the end of the 1960s most of the Robson driving staff had been indoctrinated into the strange ways of the artic and were just in time for the formal announcement of the requirement for an H.G.V. driving licence. For those drivers already in employment a procedure known as Grandfather rights allowed for an employer to sign a declaration

that his driver had been employed on a Heavy Goods Vehicle prior to the announcement date. In this way a H.G.V. licence for a permutation of Classes 1,2,3 or 4 was issued without the huge mass of currently working drivers having to undergo a test.

Robsons took their responsibility very highly in this matter and rather than glibly sign away on the declaration, they sent off one of the drivers — known to one and all as 'The Minister' — who was trained to the standard of an H.G.V. test examiner. He then spent time with a driver, riding shotgun, and if he was satisfied about his technique then the declaration was signed and the new H.G.V. licence issued.

Not everything was changed to articulated as four wheeled rigids were highly utilised on a number of traffics, not least of which was the milk work, but by the end of the 1960s this too was set for some radical change.

Working for the Milk Marketing Board had always meant agreeing to some strange rituals especially when compared to the general haulage side of Robsons work. Every year each of the Robson milk lorries would get a day long visit from a Marketing Board official who stayed with the vehicle on its day long round. A time and motion study was undertaken on each of these visits and depending on the results then a rate of payment was proffered for each specific vehicle.

With very little yearly variation in the itinerary to these vehicles it didn't create much in the way of mathematics to update the rates, but what did turn the business on its head was in the complete restructuring of how milk was to be moved at all. From the first experimental work carried out in

'Border Veteran' was bought in 1962, Stan reportedly paying about £600 for this fine example of what set him out on the transport trail. Its first big event was participating in the London to Brighton Run of 1963, but even today is still actively worked round the Vintage rally scene. The vehicle has remained in family ownership and was not part of the sale to United Glass.

As soon as the 'D' series Ford was announced, it was natural that Robsons would take them into service. This model was run for more than 10 years both in rigid and articulated form. The Joe Donaldson shot shows 'Squire' on Perth bridge heading for the canning factories around that part of Scotland for a back load of Smedleys.

the early 1960s, the trend to move milk from the farms in bulk by road tanker was being established round the country and finally came to North West England.

It was the large farmers who first invested in the new equipment needed to adopt this method of handling and whilst Robsons were approached to go into tankers, Stan sensed this was a time to consider the options. The pros to the argument included the fact that milk revenue, whilst not being excessive, was very regular.

To counteract this was the need for new investment in specialised vehicles which had a limited role and then for only a small part of the 24 hour day. The milk wagons had to be mobile for 365 days a year, a big headache when drivers' days off and holidays, plus vehicle breakdowns were borne in mind. But it was probably the booming aspect of the general haulage side of Robsons that swung the argument against continuing in this traffic as Stan realised that better productivity could be made both of his men and his machines.

The start of the 1970s saw the gradual change-over to the bulk handling of milk. The Robson platform D series Fords continued to do the round of those farmers who persevered with the churns but these were few and far between. They too had to reconsider their options and fall into line with the Milk Marketing Board policy.

It wasn't long before the 17 gallon Stocksfield 'back-breakers' were churns that were simply destined for the museum. Robsons left behind a slice of work they had been doing for close on 30 years, but it wasn't to be the only surprise that the 1970s were to reveal.

ROBSON'S HAVE WINTER LICKED WITH THE
MK II TRADER

TOUGH JOB — Ford's world-wide experience and engineering know-how are a tower of strength to Robson's Border Transport Ltd. of Carlisle. A large area of this haulage firm's territory covers the bleak heights of Shap Fell. The severe winter of 1962/3 did its worst but could not beat Robson's fleet of tough Traders from Ford.

TOUGH VEHICLE — Shown above on duty is a 7½ ton 6-cyl. diesel 160" w.b. Trader Mk II (FC), one of a fleet of 70, doing trunk runs of up to 100,000 miles per annum. 'Easy to service, in and out in no time, and *never missed a trunk run all through the cold spell*,' says Mr. Robson. 'Nothing better in this vehicle range!'

Other features of the Mk II Trader range — *Air/hydraulic brakes optional on 6-cylinder models*, 5-speed synchromesh gearbox (direct drive/overdrive options), 2-speed axle on Artic and 3-7½ ton trucks. Ford Service. Price for this model £1,251 (chassis/cab).

Today's Trader team: FC Artic (15 tons GCW); FC Truck (1½-7½ ton); 5 and 6 cu. yd. tippers; NC 1½-2 ton Vans (450 cu. ft. loadspace); 1½-7 ton NC Trucks; 1½-2-3 ton Clearway. Your Ford Main Dealer will be pleased to give you full details and a demonstration. *Tough jobs need a Thames Trader!*

THAMES TRADER
BY FORD

MADE TO LAST BY FORD OF BRITAIN Ford

Dedicated Robson followers have long been aware of the contract vehicles regularly run in the livery of Carnation. Carrying tinned milk out of their plant at Dumfries was good paying, regular work on a dedicated vehicle/driver basis. New vehicles were regularly painted up in this distinctive livery, Eric Liddle seen with his smart S34 which was to be eventually given the name of 'Emperor' when it was painted back into Robsons cream and maroon.

'Border Senior' was another of the S34 range of Fodens. To identify this type of cab, the key features are a one piece windscreen and rectangular Cibie type headlamps. The vehicle is fully loaded with tin plate, a traffic which Robsons carried a lot from the steel works of South Wales into Metal Box at Carlisle.

Although Stan was to buy out a small company who did tipper work on the rocket site of Spadeadam, this wasn't a line of work he was totally interested in. He did however regularly run a sole 4 wheel tipper, usually always called 'Tipster', that was used solely in relation to repair work round the expanding number of Robsons' sites around Carlisle. The vehicle was never used for hire and reward work.

This fine Foden was supplied new to United Glass's Castleford Depot in May 1979 by dealer Pelican Engineering of Rothwell — it's transmission being the Rolls Royce 265 engine and Fuller 9 speed gearbox. FUM 772T was to receive the name of 'Border Pageant' when it was eventually painted into a cream and maroon R.D.S. livery.

CHAPTER FIVE

Enter United Glass

At a time when Robsons were approaching their 50th anniversary, Stan was five years past the normal time when you would start to draw your old age pension. The depot was still a big attraction to him and even on a weekend he would normally pop down just for a quick look round. Now with a fleet of about 180 vehicles, Stan still got just as big a kick out of them as he did with that first Model T. A normal working day saw Stan leave his office for at least two trips round the Carlisle base. About 10 a.m. and 3 p.m. coincided with the prescribed tea breaks of the warehouse staff and this allowed Stan time to chew the cud with some of the older hands.

Those who knew Stan were aware he didn't miss much and even the quickest of glances down a line of Border vehicles was all he needed for the soundest of appraisals. The older driving staff knew that should you happen to scrape a mudguard or something like that in a tight spot, it was always best to report it straight away because there was no way that Stan would miss it. "We'll put this down to experience" was the normal Robson comment for minor indiscretions and the drivers were relieved the onslaught was nothing worse. "As long as you looked after your wagon, kept it clean and did your job proper then he never bothered you" was how Bobby Mawson related the fair way in which Stan felt about his staff.

With most of the drivers being based at Carlisle, the social aspect of such a large number meant for many organised get togethers. The only drivers who couldn't partake in these group events were those far off based shunters and due

to these vast distances, some of these were never to meet Stan in all the time they worked for him.

David 'Squeaker' Carr, who is now based at Flitwick, was an early Biggleswade man but has never been anywhere near the Carlisle depot in the 21 years he has worked for Robsons. He was to meet Stan only twice, although the first occasion was one where driver Carr was particularly fraught.

Those who know the pick-up arrangements of old worked at Covent Garden, will be aware that collecting anything up to 30 different consignments of fruit and vegetables could be particularly nerve wracking. Robsons vehicles were found to be ideal especially for traffic destined for the markets of Glasgow and Edinburgh. Being trunked up to Carlisle during the night, a 3 a.m. start by the Cumberland day man meant the fruit could be shuttled up to Scotland well in time for sale to the shop buyers making their early market rounds.

Covering such a large distance meant that scheduling was exceptionally tight, especially if the Covent Garden porters kept you waiting. Once they did come to your vehicle with all the different consignments, it was the driver's job to load them in such a fashion that they could be separately identified and thus easily unloaded north of the Border. On one particular day a combination of being kept waiting too long and then being bombarded with a deluge of irate Cockney porters provoked Squeaker to rebel as he let them know exactly what he thought of the chaotic system.

So incensed was David that he wasn't aware of two men who were watching the action. But after loading was almost complete these two approached driver Carr and intro-

'Border Tycoon' is pictured at the Haltwistle depot which although now sold back into commercial use as Mill Bridge Garage, still houses Robsons vehicles worked by long standing drivers like day man Alfie Little and night driver Harry Laidlaw. This S39 had chassis number 68820 and had come new into service on 1st January 1970.

As the late afternoon shadows lengthen, 'Hussar' is seen coming back into the Carlisle depot fully loaded for the night driver to take over. This S39 tractor unit dates from 1st October 1969 and was one of the lightest of the marque, tipping the scales at 4 ton 19cwt. 88 lbs. It was chassis number 68420, being fitted with the Gardner 6LXB engine.

duced themselves as his employers, they being Stan Robson and George Flenley. Following complaints that had filtered back from the shunters, they had decided to come south to witness themselves the problems of loading in the 'Garden'. David hadn't to explain the reasons behind him blowing up as both Stan and George knew the pressures the shunter worked under. Whilst Robsons provided an ideal service for the Scottish bound fruit, it wasn't long before they stopped collecting here, as management agreed the scheduling couldn't live with such inbuilt frustrations.

In many respects the Robson business was a highly thought of concern and that's not just amongst other hire and reward companies. The fact that at one time over 300 names appeared on the waiting list of prospective drivers gives some indication of how they were accepted amongst the staff side in the North West of England.

The firm had been able to create a warm feeling around itself prompted by continuity of good service by long-standing staff, although in some ways they had been obliged to accept change. Stan had never had many strong feelings about the Union, but like many other similar haulage concerns, he had been almost forced to ensure drivers had joined. In some places where the Unions had total dominance — like the docks a driver had to be a card carrying Union member or his vehicle wouldn't be allowed access to get unloaded.

Negotiating changes in pay and conditions at Robsons had been done at a very personal level of the Company which resulted in satisfaction being gained for both sides. It thus came as particularly painful for both drivers and the Com-

pany, that both became heavily embroiled in the national drivers' strike of 1976/77.

The Robson men knew they would obviously get at least the going rate of whatever was nationally decided as Stan made this clear from the outset, but this dispute was influenced by forces way beyond the control of both staff and employers at Carlisle. The Union had targeted hire and reward operations throughout the country for strike action, leaving own account hauliers to carry on undisturbed with their own vehicle operations. If this wasn't complicated enough, the situation was confused even further by the Union issuing dispensations to certain hauliers who gave undertakings that they would pay whatever the agreed rate was, when the dispute finally ended. For small concerns, these dispensations made all the difference between survival and actually going out of business. The ironic part to these verbal agreements with the Union was that in some isolated cases the haulier went back on his word. The result was that even though their respective drivers had been allowed to work during the strike, they were never actually paid the agreed rate when it was finished.

With Robsons being such a high profile concern in the hire and reward field they were targeted by both sides of the argument. Even though they agreed quite openly to pay whatever was decided, the Union declined to issue the asked for dispensations. On the other side, the Road Haulage Association were exerting pressure on Robsons to stand firm and not concede to the demands, for if a nationally accepted name like Robsons Border were to give in, then many others would naturally follow.

(Above) *One of the most pleasing loads for many of the Robsons drivers were the square cut bales of paper pulp. Loaded up to about 6" from the end of the semi-trailer and running down its centre, the 32 ton gross vehicle always seemed to have a beautiful balance about it. WHH 869K was chassis number 74000 and was fitted with the Gardner 6LXB engine. It dates from 1st October 1971.*

(Left) *Name buffs will note the significance in coupling sister vehicles 'Border Nimrod' to 'Border Searcher'. Both in fact were never to receive fleet numbering as they fell out of fleet step by starting life in the dedicated contract livery of Carnations. The Geoff Milne photograph shows 'Searcher' on the pumps at Carlisle with a load of waste paper. Both these S39s entered service in late 1970.*

Liverpudlian Ray Jenkins was to take this photograph of 'Border Prince' one day but he never dreamt that the same vehicle would end up as being preserved by good friend Robert Chicken. The S39 is now restored back into as new condition, it first going on to the road in June 1972. It did at times work the Biggleswade trunk, one of its regular day shunters being David 'Squeaker' Carr.

With the S20 eight wheeler version of 'Border Unicorn' being sold off into showland service, the same name was put onto this S39 tractor unit which came into service on 1st September 1972. Pictured in the heart of Edinburgh, chassis number 76780 is hauling a load of glass bottles destined for delivery off the bottom of Princes Street.

'Border Courage' had Tommy Mooney as its regular driver although one of the fleet fitters is seen shunting the vehicle at Carlisle. The inboard clean lines of the sheeted load indicates a cargo of pulp probably collected from one of the North East ports. This S39 had chassis number 74896 and came new into service on 1st Jan. 1972.

Not a great deal of weight, but this load of scaffolding required fastidious care with securing. Robsons did a lot of this type of traffic, especially up into the Glasgow area. 'Border Neptune' is Foden S39, chassis number 76784, it going into service on 1st October 1972. The tractor had an unladen weight of 5 ton 3cwt. 75lbs and had a 9'6" wheelbase.

Strikes of any kind rarely produce winners. What seemed like an eternity, but which was hardly a month, finally produced an agreement. Vehicles got back to work and after a few days, on the surface at least, things were back to normal and it was though the strike had never happened. But to some, the effects of the dispute had gone much deeper, and to 70 year old Stan it had cut through him like a knife. In all his 50 years in haulage he had never encountered a situation where he had been dictated to like that and he vowed it was a situation that would never be repeated.

In essence Stan sensed that he was getting too old to go through heart breaking phases like this and like many times before in his life, he had to sit back and consider his options. The alternatives weren't many as Stan realised that he had enjoyed quite a good innings in his three score years and ten. But the mental decision to sell up as a going concern was probably the best he could make, even though to a man who had dedicated his life to his transport fleet, it should have been unthinkable. What Stan couldn't bear thinking about, should he die, was the prospect of his beloved 'Border' fleet being decimated as his estate was carved up for death duties.

This wasn't the first occasion that Stan had bucked what was in essence a Robson system. It had probably seemed unthinkable to specify anything but Foden as the fleet flag-ship, but during the 1970s, the type of vehicle in use had come very much under the spotlight. Although Fodens continued to be bought in large numbers, Stan felt uneasy in the way that this company was producing their products.

The European importers led by Volvo, from as early as

1968, and then Scania, were offering an entirely different new concept both in vehicle design and performance together with a high standard of driver comforts. Some of these new tractors like the Volvo F86 were also exceptionally light for their high gross ratings, so in deciding to try out the new offerings, Robson opted for the DAF 2200 as their first trial import. 'Border Consul' and 'Border Cyclone' were the first two DAFs to go into operation as per the Company fleet list, and rather befitting the latter's name, the marque was set to take the Company by storm.

At the outset the 2200s were specifically bought to bridge the gap between the lightweight Ford and the heavy-weight Fodens, it being the S80 range that was in production at the mid point of the 1970s. But the Robson specification for the early Dafs — and for many more to come — saw them into service not fitted with a traditional European full sleeper cab, but simply in very short day cab form.

The philosophy behind this specification was built up from several reasons. Both Stan Robson and George Flenley agreed that they were perhaps old fashioned in their reason-ing, but they felt quite strongly that once a man finished his day of work then he shouldn't be expected to spend his night time cocooned in the same habitat. You wouldn't expect, they argued, an engineer to curl up beside his lathe inside his sleeping bag to pass the darkened hours after his day of work. No, a lorry driver too, needed a complete break away from his vehicle and working environment, so that he could return the next day fully rested and ready for a good day's work.

This main argument against the sleeper cab may have

'Border Knight' was another Foden which stayed around for a long time, being chopped from an eight wheeled platform to a four wheeled tractor. This Michael Cook photograph showing the vehicle on shunting duties in 1974. Parked next to it is the ex Ronnie Yates coil carrying trailer that Geordie Graham's 'Border Eagle' ran on this type of traffic out of Ravenscraig.

flown in the face of convention as many drivers from other Continental vehicle users tended to prefer using the sleeper cab rather than risk using some overnight digs which may have questionable reputations. But Robsons weren't concerned about what others did, they reserved the right to work things out for themselves and they were also swayed by the legal argument against sleeper cabs. It was a fact that for many years — right up until the overall length limit of artics was increased to 15.5 metres — that tractor units fitted with a full sleeper cab could rarely couple to a standard 40ft. semi-trailer and stay within the Construction and Use Regulation length limit of 15 metres. There was a saving to be made both in unladen weight and in initial cost which all added to strengthen the Robson resolve in favouring the fitment of day cabs.

With or without sleepers, the DAFs soon reaped huge driver acceptance. The Foden/Gardner combination had given a standard of reliability that was second to none but talk to any of their drivers, and they would probably tell you that they were noisy, draughty and uncomfortable. If they had a choice about changing anything they would probably opt to replace the hydraulically operated throttle pedal with something far lighter and less painful to the right knee. Biggleswade man David Carr recalls that some drivers even removed the hefty throttle return spring to try and ease the amount of pressure that was needed for maximum performance, but it didn't have much effect.

Getting the optimum from the Foden 12 speed gearbox was also a work of art. The main floor mounted four speed lever was easy enough to locate into cog but the fascia

(Right) 'Border Merlin', also loaded with waste paper, is seen southbound on the M6 in 1975. George Kilpatrick was the vehicle's regular driver, it coming into service on 1st April 1974. No fool in performance however, as the Rolls Royce 220 powered vehicle was recalled as being quite a goer. The tractor has been saved for preservation and is now part of the Robert Chicken collection.

(Below) There may be those who remark that 'Border Samson' was a crude defiling conversion of the original S18 eight wheeler 'Border Courier'. But those of the fitting staff at Carlisle who worked and loved the vehicle reckon that when it was in its crane/recovering guise that the Foden did its' best work for Robsons.

To coincide with the U.K's entry into the Common Market, Stan coined the name 'Europa' to go onto the first of the Foden S80s to come to Carlisle. This vehicle came into service on 1st June 1973, with its regular driver being Jimmy Dicker. The Geoff Milne photograph taken at Carlisle sees it loaded with waste paper destined for delivery to Purfleet in Essex.

mounted three speed range change shift lever was extremely delicate to position. Move it slightly past the intermediate range position by mistake and the next change would find the whole transmission dropping into neutral as the vehicle slowed to a stop.

DAF were also to offer a 12 speed gearbox, but with a six speed main box coupled to a two speed splitter, all the differing ratios were selected by a combination of the left hand and its fingers. This left hand was kept busy, for instead of hav-ing the slow long lugging Gardner that would pull and pull no matter what the revs of the engine, the DAF — like many of the smaller similar lightweight European imports — relied on a small engine that had to be kept revving freely to produce its best performance. Perhaps it was a bit of a flashback to the days of the Foden two stroke, albeit with less of the unpredictability and with — sadly to some — far less of the charismatic noise.

Although bought initially as a middleweight, Robsons soon found their DAFs capable of doing the same job as the heavyweight Fodens. Following on to buy the slightly bigger DAF 2800s underlined the Robson acceptance of the Dutch marque, which soon proved its intention of sharing the flagship mantle with that of Foden. Being prepared to re-assess your vehicle base, even in the face of 40 years of historical good service from Foden, augured well for Robsons and underlined the Company's awareness to matters.

Whilst Stan didn't naturally trumpet the gut tearing decision that he had made to sell out, he mentally resolved to look for a buyer that was suitable to him and not just the other way round. With a long list of established customers serviced

In 1972 there was a major shake up in the Leyland Group with Albion changing its name to Leyland (Glasgow). Their products also saw a change of cab with this Clydesdale 24ton tractor unit using the 'G' type cab that Leyland had inherited from the old BMC FJ series. Robsons tried a quartet of these new 'Albions', Geoff Milne's photograph taken on 23rd February 1974 pictures their ex demonstrator 'Clipper'.

by a 180 strong fleet that now offered huge warehousing facilities at Kirkbride, Robsons would have been a large jewel in anyone's transport crown. Both the National Freight Consortium and the Transport Development Group had made it clear that they wished to buy out Robsons, whilst Stan had also made it clear that he wasn't interested in either of them as possible suitors. In fact the decision to sell had to be put on ice for a couple of years, as Stan had to wait until 1979 before he talked to a man called Nettleship.

At that time Herbert Nettleship had been with United Glass for 14 years, a period during which he had completely transformed the distribution side of the U.G. business. Joining the Company in '65 from British Coal, his open brief under the title of Group Distribution Manager had been to radically sort out the strange inheritance which embraced the U.G. distribution network.

First formed about 1909, the passage of time had seen United Glass (Bottle Manufacturers) expand to embrace 13 different concerns throughout the U.K. These stretched from Alloa Glass in the Scottish heartland down to Key Glass at Harlow in Essex. Although having only two or three trucks of their own at this time, the Group relied on sub contractors to move their products which included for many years, big use of the British rail network.

The main so-called asset to the U.G. distribution network, was in having 152 different warehouses, spread country wide, which included no less than 42 of these being located in Scotland. Varying in shape, size and even general condition, some of this odd collection even had railway lines

'Border Terrier' was another Leylandised version of the Albion Clydesdale, this shot taken on 6th July 1974 shows the vehicle as a four wheel platform vehicle. Ronnie Burridge was its regular driver in this form as a long distance vehicle but the chassis was to be converted into a van for Jimmy 'Ginger' Ivison to drive on cloth work.

*'Border Venture'
was new to
Robsons on 1st
July 1976, it
having the Rolls
Royce Eagle 265
bhp engine.
Chassis number
94316 is seen
loaded with
bagged fertiliser
destined for
storage at the
Kirkbride
warehousing
complex. Collected
from the Nitram
plant at ICI
Billingham,
Robsons then
acted as a
distribution point
in the North West
on behalf of ICI as
people like West
Cumberland
Farmers would
draw their required
loads out of the
Robson store.*

*Not a vehicle to appear on the Robson fleet list,
or even just a demonstrator, JAO 446N was
actually a Scania 111 operated by owner/driver
William Ivinson. Based at Welton near
Caldbeck, the Scania did at times provide
traction under Robsons own trailers, but is here
pictured carrying a Robsons load using an
Ivinson owned semi.*

running through them as an indication to the normal mode of delivery. These glass storage points had been created on the reasoning that wherever U.G. had a customer, then they would also have a warehouse very close to the final delivery point. Such an arrangement ensured that the customer could be supplied very quickly from his own particular stock pile, of his own particular glass product.

With the vast improvement in the U.K. road network, such a necessity of service became out of date. For in the strides taken in road haulage the overnight trunk system meant that an order placed one day could both in theory and in practice, be delivered the next day. Herbert Nettleship thus found it as part of his remit to streamline this dated concept, where these vast number of U.G. outposts were gradually replaced with more modern facilities but this time at the place of glass manufacture, not at the place of delivery.

It was not only on the distribution side of affairs that United Glass was set to radically change. From being a Public Limited Company in 1966, ownership had been taken on a 50/50 basis between the two shareholders of Distillers Co. Ltd and Owens of Illinois, the biggest glass people in the world. Owens were to provide the new Group Managing Director, Bill Spengler, and under his guidance a new team of management set to on the streamlining of United Glass operations. Along the way Nettleship was able to demonstrate to some of the older glass making men how it could be far more viable to run your own fleet of vehicles for deliveries, so sub-contractors like J & A Smith of Maddiston — who ran 39 vehicles exclusively out of Alloa — had to look elsewhere for traffic.

Not the first of the DAFs to be bought by Robsons, 'Border Kestrel' was actually the fourth of these 2200 tractor units, this one coming into service on 1st November 1975. Perhaps of equal excitement to the Robson drivers — John Templetown just escaping out of shot — was the godsend of the curtain sided trailer.

It had been in Scotland that Nettleship created his first transport region, with its Transport Manager Bill Lindsay setting up in rather modest premises in a shed at Clackmannan. With glass movements being so intensely localised to a small area of Scotland, having vehicles of their own — rather than continually hiring in all sorts of transport — soon scythed away at the heavy sub contractors costings that United Glass had accepted at what they thought was the norm. Repeating this Scottish experiment to create four other regional transport areas meant that by 1974, the distribution bill of U.G. had been reduced from 20% to 9% of the sales turnover.

In all five regional centres, the United Glass slice of moving their own products remained very much on a local regional level. Nettleship decided that taking the next step of hauling glass destined for long distance delivery could only be done if suitable return traffic was found. United Glass may have been able to create some of their own back loads of glass although in some regions this was always going to be difficult and generally speaking it was never going to be enough. The continued reliance on sub contractors to move this long distance traffic underlined the fact that it could be a financial mistake for U.G. vehicles to take this traffic on, if the return journey had to be done empty.

Cutting down on unladen running was a problem that the hire and reward side of the road haulage industry had to surmount on a daily basis. But to bring this class of expertise into the United Glass empire, Nettleship sensed that it would be most expeditious if the expertise was bought in. His Board agreed and Nettleship was given the authority to

'Border Swallow' was one of a quartet of Volvo F86 tractor units that Robson bought from the Nicholas Elliott concern about June 1977 when that concern decided to sell up. Elliotts ran in a green based livery and were based at Haltwistle doing a lot of work out of the BXL factory. Although the Volvos were to be moved across to Carlisle fairly soon after purchase, Foden driver Dessy Bright described his one ride in a Volvo as being beautifully smooth.

Key Glassworks was one of the many concerns that were to form the consortium of United Glass, Key being taken over about 1962. Although Key ran about six vehicles of their own at this time, the 1964 registered Thames Trader seen at Harlow is believed to be a contract vehicle run by Spurlings.

(Below) *Having a red based livery, Landrover 'Border Bantam' was part of the job lot when Robsons acquired the Volvo fleet from Nicholas Elliott. The Geoff Milne photograph shows the vehicle at Haltwistle on 2nd September 1978, but the vehicle was soon clawed over to Carlisle for use as a fitter's runabout.*

seek out a suitable hire and reward haulier to buy into the U.G. empire.

Gaining outline permission to proceed in this fashion may have been a big step forward, but Nettleship knew that converting it into tangible action was not going to be that easy. But had he needed to underline the importance of transport and warehousing a screaming demand for glass in the mid 1970s meant that U.K. production could not keep up with the huge order book. The newly created chain of U.G. warehouses and road going fleet was thus kept extremely busy absorbing the vast amount of glass that had to be imported from the Continent before being delivered on to the customer.

Surmounting these logistical problems with a fleet of close to 200 strong, meant Nettleship had to put the acquisition plan on the back burner for a couple of years, but by about 1978 the search began again in earnest. He first approached the two sub contractors who were doing the most work for United Glass — both well known, highly respected hire & reward concerns, but both politely declined the tentative offer. However, right out of the blue Nettleship received a phone call from Stan Robson. The grapevine message had filtered down to Durranhill Industrial Estate that United Glass were looking to buy something suitable. Robsons did do a small amount of work for U.G. especially out of the St. Helens depot in Lancashire. Although Herbert knew both Stan and George Flenley very well, he hadn't approached them to think of selling as the vibrations he had sensed were that they would have turned him down. That one telephone

call was thus to decide the future for both Robsons and the United Glass distribution arm.

"Herbert, I like the cut of your jib. I'd like our Company to get into bed with yours" was the recalled remarks that came as quite a surprise to Nettleship who admitted that he would be interested in buying out Robsons. With Stan at last finding someone he would like to sell to, the tentative discussions between both parties commenced. Done obviously in circumstances of complete confidentiality, the agreed decision to buy/sell and even the price involved was established at a fairly early stage. The administration and sheer bureaucracy involved meant that about 18 months were to elapse before the deal was finalised.

That period of 1979-80 also heralded one of the worst recessions of modern times that both road transport and industry had to endure. The decision both on the price involved and even whether to buy Robsons at all was questioned by senior U.G. management, but Nettleship stated that he had given his word, the deal would go through.

3rd November 1980 was an historic day in the Robsons calendar and it was perhaps rather fitting that the transaction involving Robsons Border Transport took place at 'Wrayside' in the home and heartland of Stan Robson. Two million, one hundred thousand pounds changed hands at the slip of a pen which made Stan Robson and the small number of previous shareholders in the Border Company, rather wealthy people.

The day was also to herald the end of the O'Reilly involvement. True, he had stayed as a founder shareholder in Robsons Border Transport Ltd, but N.T's involvement had

(Below) *Another second-hand purchase, but this time in early 1978, were a quintet of ERFs and a single Foden from the company of J.W. Hodgson of Carlisle. This Gardner 180 powered 'A' series ERF had been name 'Solway Pride' in its earlier Hodgson's days. It wasn't surprising that Stan was to name the first two of these ex Hodgson ERFs as 'Soldier' and 'Sailor'. 35 years earlier when he had bought two second-hand ERF four wheelers from the Pratt brothers, these were the names he had given to those two vehicles.*

(Left) This fine quartet of Fodens' respective first regular drivers were 771 — Fred Fletcher, 772 — Alan Hartley, 773 —Harry Johnson, and 774 — Alan Hepworth.

(Right) Pictured new when it came to United Glass's Harlow depot in January 1980, CJM 752V is chassis number 41740. It was to receive the name of 'Border Salute' when painted cream and maroon, it working mainly out of the R.D.S. Flitwick depot. It is currently endings its' days as a shunter based at Wellsbourne.

It was a refreshing aspect to Robson followers that second-hand vehicles, like this ERF four wheeler, would occasionally appear almost without warning. Prior to 1968 many second-hand vehicles were bought simply to obtain their carrier's licence, but once 'A', 'B' and 'C' licensing was discontinued, this transferring practice wasn't possible. It was thus sometimes a mystery why vehicles like 'Seagull' were ever bought. She flew into Carlisle about August 1979 being chassis number 18912.

been far more than just drawing up the yearly accounts. Administration, right down to the drivers' wages, is a term that might explain the large slice of O'Reilly's influence on Robsons. However, with the huge machinery of United Glass set to take over, these long standing, if somewhat uniquely quaint business arrangements, were set to change. The O'Reilly accountancy firm would never be quite the same again.

It was, however, a particularly sad day for Stan to endure. Whilst George Flenley and all of the other Robson staff remained with the Company just as before, Stan had to completely sever all the connections he had forged with his fleet over the last 54 years. A small piece of paper with a meaninglessly large amount of money written on it was thus exchanged for a whole way of life, and stomaching it was not particularly palatable.

For a 74 year old man, accepting the consequences of his decision took some doing, as his name, his old vehicles and their treasured 'Border' names were still an everyday sight, especially around Carlisle. To accept that these were now simply a part of the United Glass Group stuck in the Robson throat, although as far as the Company of Robsons Border Transport was concerned, it was arguably in all the circumstances, the best thing that could have happened. In the period of deep recession that followed many huge transport companies had to retract quite extensively to stave off possible extinction. Although the Robsons of old were destined to endure huge restructuring in the years that followed, their continuity was assured and their contribution to the distribution industry destined to accelerate.

Pictured outside R.B.T. headquarters in Carlisle, this Haulmaster was the last Foden to carry the revered 'Princess' name. Loaded with superfine aluminium powder, the traffic may appear fairly bulky but it is also fairly light. Robsons were to carry this type of cargo from Burnt Island, Kirkcaldy, to all parts of the country.

CHAPTER SIX

Towards the 21st century

Although it took more than a year of administrative hard work to sort out compatible mating arrangements for Robsons Border Transport and the United Glass transport/warehousing interests, it was in no way a period of stagnation. Most important person to any haulier is the customer and the Robson/U.G. management team had to ensure that all the old 'Border' customers were kept fully updated with the dramatic developments, but more importantly assured that the high level of service was to remain, and if anything, be improved on.

The staff of the two concerns were naturally conscious of what might happen, for, as elsewhere in the industry, the own account United Glass people had always had a far better pay structure than the hire and reward concerns like Robsons. Obtaining parity between the two fixed lines would mean almost walking a tightrope but with thorough continuous negotiations with all the Unions involved, the details were finalised. Herbert Nettleship recalled that his plan was set to take three years for the two sides to totally intermesh, but with close co-operation from all parties, the plan was finalised in only two years.

The coming together of two companies in a merger like this was best served by the creation of an entirely new company, which meant new contracts of employment for all the staff involved. This meant the 'buying out' of certain rights — especially on the U.G. side — but those who didn't wish to accept the hammered out proposals could obviously avail themselves of the more than generous redundancy procedure terms that United Glass offered for all group personnel. As a guide-

stick these terms were worth three times as much as the Government had laid down as redundancy payments in these circumstances. In the throes of a recession however, it's not surprising that only a few staff opted for these large cash handshakes.

Deciding on a name for this new company was perhaps more difficult and after prolonged boardroom discussions the previously used name for the transport/warehousing division of U.G - United Distribution Services - was the one that was agreed upon. It's not surprising that the United Glass management wished the 'United' name to be dominant in their road going fleet. But Managing Director of this new Division, Herbert Nettleship, knew that his projected goal had always been to make a bold impact on the hire and reward market. He had fought strongly against his board in this respect, he being in favour of using the name of Robsons. It was to be this name he felt, that could give the new concern credibility in this particular field. Whilst he may have lost this argument in the first instance, what he did get his board to concede was in adopting the Robsons' style of cream and maroon livery for the new vehicles.

However, following continued Nettleship pressure, the life of U.D.S. was short lived and by December 1984 it was to be Robsons Distribution Services that was the agreed banner. A name which is still in use today, it should be noted that at that time, as per the fine print on the bottom of the Company letter head, this was not a limited company in its own right, but a trading division of United Glass Ltd. The colours remained as per the Robson livery, whilst the tradition of

'Border Valiant' is perhaps a fitting name to NHH 658W for, taking to the road on 1st April 1981, it was to be the last Foden bought new by Robsons. After buying from this Sandbach factory for almost 44 years, the chain was to be finally broken. John Jackson was the usual roamer driver of this Haulmaster which had chassis number 106966. It is loaded with reels of paper out of Thames Board at Workington.

'Border' names was retained — and obviously extended on to the ex U.G. vehicles — as was a system of fleet numbering.

Although it is now discontinued, Robsons had always followed a rather unique system of numbering their fleet. As well as using a consecutive number, Robsons had always prefixed this by two or more letters. The letters were in fact initials, with FD standing for Foden Diesel and DD for DAF Diesel, the first letter indentifying the marque, the second the type of fuel used. Finding something different to a diesel driven truck is quite difficult, although the pre-nationalisation list notes a few petrol powered vehicles, so Stan obviously decided that the letter/number system had some merit, which prompted him to adopt it in those heady days of 1936.

The theory of such a system was straight forward but the practical application obviously had to absorb the Tommy Osgood factor. Following Jimmy Hornsby into the Company as chief painter/signwriter took some doing, but slogans like 'Robsons Frae Carlisle' were an Osgood conception. There weren't too many vans in the fleet of old, but what were, plus the demountable containers that Robsons used quite profusely, were a signwriter's Utopia. Slogans like 'Here comes Robsons' written on the front facing part of the body were always following by 'There goes Robsons' painted on the rear. Studying older photographs reveals joyous observations of the signwriters flair like 'Robsons. Always a Move Ahead' or 'Robsons Transport Services Always Moving.'

Osgood had his own little way of deciding on what make a vehicle might be and whilst the Ford four wheelers that Robsons used aplenty should really have had an F prefix

A bit of a rarity in the guise of an Ergomatic Albion in Robsons colours was HVD 646L which dates from 1972. The vehicle came to Carlisle as a platform vehicle, reputedly from a United Glass source. The fitting staff at Robsons have developed a huge expertise in engineering, and fitting the van body was, for them, a fairly easy exercise.

United Distribution Services in cream and maroon was a livery that featured on only a few of the Robsons/ U.G. vehicles and then for only a very short time. Seen coupled to the special sand tipping trailer that works into United Glass's Alloa plant, this Seddon Atkinson 401 was new in November 1982. To be based at Glenrothes, the tractor received the name 'Border Glory' when repainted into the full R.D.S livery.

(Below) Sharing the same 'Border Badger' name, this Seddon Atkinson 200 also shares the fact that it came to Carlisle as a second-hand flat before having the van body built onto it by Robsons staff. The vehicle dates from December 1978, it being chassis number 67222. Arnold Stobbard was the rigid's normal driver tending to work the Cumberland area on delivery/collection small load work.

to the fleet number, Tommy usually put a T in to denote Thames. Of course Fodens were used in similarly large numbers so the point could be argued that Tommy adopted the T letter rather than be confused if both Fords and Fodens were prefixed with the letter F.

In a rapidly expanding fleet, creating individual touches like this was a pleasurable diversion but sometimes Tommy's individuality could be very frustrating. He thought nothing of it to give two different vehicles the same fleet number and then perhaps leave a gap of say three numbers that weren't allocated to anything. For reasons best known to himself he could, of course, issue a vehicle with a new fleet number if it came in for a repaint or even give it a new name. If taken to task about his methods, the somewhat cheeky schoolboy grin as a response would reflect his feelings. But whilst the early numbering of Robsons vehicles might have had the odd 'Osgood' hiccup, what happened when the old United Glass fleet were eventually brought under the Robsons banner was a list maker's nightmare.

It just so happened that the United Glass vehicles had also been fleet numbered in a similar fashion to Robsons, and at the time of the merger the current fleet were using numbers in the region of 600-700. This of course, coincided with some numberings then in use at Robsons, so the decision was made to re-allocate the applicable Robson vehicles, moving them up into the 700-800 numbering phase.

Whilst this administrative move had very little in the way of practical implications, what soon became apparent was in how the smaller Robson vehicles were weeded out of the

'Border Sapphire' was new to United Glass in January 1980, it being chassis number 41913. Pictured at the Harlow depot in September 1986, the ERF is fitted with the Rolls Royce 265 engine. The site of what was the Robson base at Harlow on the side of the United Glass plant has been sold and now houses as supermarket. The R.D.S. operations at Harlow are now based inside the U.G. plant. 'Sapphire' is currently engaged on shunting duties at St. Helens.

'Border Titan' was ERF chassis number 44667 and new to United Glass's Castleford depot in March 1981. It ran until 1989 when an undetected water leak in its Cummins 240 engine brought its' trunking life with Robsons towards an end. It was used as a yard shunter at Castleford for a while before being sold to Eddie Timmins at Sandbach. The engine was repaired before the vehicle was sold on again, to Ireland.

fleet and the emphasis put on to maximum weight artics running at 32 tons. The large Robson roaming contingent of old was set to be pruned as a dictate from the new management for stronger discipline in operations, but as workhorses for this new line of work, the Robson experiences stood the new R.D.S. in good stead for what vehicles were finally adopted.

When first entering transport about 1970, the distribution division of United Glass had followed overtures from their shareholders to fly the flag and buy British. With a dominance of localised operations, the choice for motive power was to be the Leyland Mastiff — which had a 26 ton gross rating — coupled to a 33ft. flat semi-trailer. However, like many other operators, U.G. suffered huge problems with the Leyland of that era, at times having traumatic downtime that did reach up to 30% of a vehicle's operational life.

The problems were finally solved but the effects had been felt, and Nettleship vowed never to buy Leyland again. In fairness some Guy Big J's that were run gave fairly good service — heavy steering apart — but the Company was finally to change over to Scania and became the biggest user of this Swedish marque in Scotland during the mid 1970s. Strangely it was very bad service — to the North of England section of the fleet — that soured Scania use, so U.G. then turned to a Sandbach mixture of ERF and Foden by the time of the Robson merger.

The start of the 1980s saw a consolidation of the two fleets, but by the time it came round to invest in new vehicles, it was the DAF 2800 that was to be strongly favoured with Scania 112s and ERFS also taken in large numbers. An air of

discipline was also extended into the vehicle investment programme, the days of the strange second-hand vehicles appearing on a Robson whim were long gone.

But distribution on the huge scale in which Robsons found themselves involved — their warehousing is now measured in millions of square feet — is far more than just their proud fleet of 'Border' vehicles. It is probably the influences that were championed by Herbert Nettleship which prompted changes of attitude towards the humble pallet, the design and operation of the fork lift truck, the removal of the rave — the small prominence on the side of the old fashioned vehicle body — but more importantly the conception and demand of development of the curtainsider, which had the most effect on distribution operations.

It was to be United Glass's birth into transport which made the necessity for the curtainsider scream for attention. With the predominance of short haul journeys into Scotland, it was frustrating for both drivers and management to have to spend hours in sheeting and roping a load secure, only to be stripping it down a very short time later.

Nettleship had first struggled with this dilemma when he had joined the company in '65 and was dealing with the time being spent on this procedure by his sub-contractors. Working with John French of Spurlings, a curtain sided trailer was constructed, but problems with strength and rigidity, plus basic curtain operation, meant this early prototype was a disaster.

But the seed was planted and United Glass Chief Engineer Jack Sankey was tasked in getting someone to

Having the single piece windscreen 'Border Diplomat' is an example of the Fleetmaster tractor unit which was new to United Glass in May 1981. Having the chassis number 110330, the vehicle was normally based at the Glenrothes depot. Providing traction to a Towmaster trailer, the photograph illustrates a poignant point to later developments in the Robson story.

'Border Bastion' is chassis number 108374 and was also new to United Glass in February 1981. Seen at its normal base of Castleford, it was run by Robsons North Region until 1989. It was also sold to dealer Timmins at Sandbach who sold it on again and the vehicle is believed to be still running, based in the Midlands.

invent the ideal curtain sided trailer. Fellow own account hauliers Watney's the brewers were also on the same trail so the combination approached Gerald Broadbent of Boalloy and the birth of the Tautliner was soon in the offing.

Today, with so many variations of the Tautliner in daily use, life without this type of trailer/vehicle bodywork seems like a nightmare. Fifteen years on from those pioneering days in the late 1960s, the Robson men were to have the highest regard of that time saving concept. "One of the greatest things every invented," says recently retired driver Dessy Bright. "The only difficulty you had was hanging on to it, for if you had to leave your trailer at Carlisle for some reason, then sure as anything someone would try and grab it because they were that good." Currently, with a figure of about 270 curtainsiders, it still means that Robsons run about 200 platform semi-trailers, which of course require roping/sheeting in the conventional manner, as and when the load dictates.

Dessy Bright had lived and worked for all his Robson service first out of Gilsland and then out of the Haltwistle depot. To the Head Office at Kingston Road in Staines, Middlesex, this small staging post was hardly noticeable on the map, so Bright, like the other Haltwistle men, were naturally concerned as to their future as the basis of Robsons operations were slowly changed.

The Haltwistle men needn't have worried for the evolution saw a regional structure devised, similar to that adopted in those early United Glass days. But, limited to four regions, the divisional breakdown saw 'Scottish' based at Alloa, 'Borders' at Carlisle, 'Northern' at St. Helens and

As a name 'Goliath' first adorned a 1948 Coles 6 ton electric crane which came to Robsons in a weathered condition from T. M. Hartley, Ullswater Sawmills, Penrith. A better recipient of the title must have been this 'C' type ERF, chassis number 48874, which had Dave Connelly as its regular driver. Starting off in day cab form, it went onto Carnation work, but also had a small Jennings made sleeper cab attached. The ERF is currently based at Alloa.

'Border Cadet' is sister vehicle to 'Border Comet' — YCP 175Y — both coming new to United Glass at their Castleford depot. 'Cadet' has chassis number 74644 and was put on the road in October 1982, its first regular driver being Ralph Williamson. Fitted with the Rolls Royce 265 engine, the vehicle found favour with the Castleford staff, although it is currently based at St. Helens.

'Southern' region based in Flitwick. Vehicles were also operated out of depots at Harlow, Durham, Glenrothes plus many other places like Haltwistle, although the lay-by structure at Biggleswade was terminated and staff offered work across at Flitwick. All the newly employed Robsons staff had to adapt to the changing patterns of their work but perhaps the biggest transition to any of the operating bases of R.D.S. was that which was performed at the 'Northern' depot of Castleford.

Like all the Robsons network, the base at Castleford has an excellent location, this depot being close to the M62/ A1 junction in West Yorkshire. Castleford had been a long established glass manufacturing plant on a 28 acre site but following the big downturn in demand for glass in the late 1970s recession, the decision was made to end production to stave off even more losses. Even clearing the site for future development was deemed to be too uneconomic as it meant large scale demolition of huge chimneys, furnaces and even a blacksmith's shop. The first quotes for site clearance saw figures of hundreds of thousands of pounds being mentioned, which was totally off-putting to the United Glass board, especially at a time when money was so tight.

With glass making at an end, Robsons Distribution Services had continued to run a small fleet out of the Castleford premises but Regional Manager Richard Porter sensed there was a lot more potential in this decaying site. His enthusiasm convinced the Robson management who in turn decided to buy the site from its United Glass parent.

Three years on from then, the demolition was done — at a far more competitive price than first quoted — new access

'Border Regent' is DAF 2800 chassis number 249454, coming on fleet in March 1984. Although based for a time at the Durham depot, it is seen coupled to the sole tipping trailer based in Carlisle. The trailer is normally placed in the premises of Nestles at Dalston where it is filled with scrap bits of tin coming off the canning process. Once or twice a week the trailer is hauled across to the North East where it is unloaded at a scrap dealers in Hartlepool.

The Robson dedication to day cab fitment on their artic tractor units prompted some different looking vehicles, the Volvo F10 appearing strangely short when seen in this guise. 'Javelin' was the first of only four Volvo F10 tractors taken into service. This one bears chassis number 25308, it was first registered in December 1983, and currently works out of the St. Helens depot.

'Robsons frae Carlisle' was a slogan that painter Tommy Osgood conceived but the times have long gone since strange expressions of the painters' delight appeared on the side of the fleet's van bodies. One of the best must have been the flying stork which is carrying a baby, supported in a nappy, slung 'hammock' style. The words printed round the pair read 'Trust Robsons with precious loads'. 'Border Valour' is chassis number 252229 and is currently based at St. Helens.

roads were laid, and more importantly, 13,000 square metres of improved warehousing created. A spin off to local businesses saw them given the opportunity to rent some of the smaller buildings that Robsons couldn't make use of in an area of Castleford now known as the Acorn Industrial Estate.

Although the changes at Castleford were rather unique, what wasn't surprising was the high standing that Robsons laid claim to in their field of distribution. It had taken just over four years, but by early 1985, Herbert Nettleship was able to sit back and reap the praise that was given to R.D.S. Perhaps it was all the more sweeter when it came from a man who had been an early critic of what was being done to his cosseted conception.

Stan Robson may have cut the umbilical cord in November 1980 when he sold up, but it didn't mean he had no concern for his old business. With grandson Gary Hutchinson being promoted to the Regional Manager's post at Carlisle, Stan still had a firm line of communication from Durranhill Road. But having managed your own concern for 54 years it stuck in the throat to admire someone who had set to and changed a lot that you had conceived. Although by 1985 Stan was ready to admit his inner feelings and congratulate Herbert for what he had been able to achieve.

These five years in retirement had not seen Stan blessed with the best of luck. Never the fittest of men, a fall on the ice which badly damaged his hip, started a further decline in health, and meant walking in his latter years was only done painfully with the aid of a stick.

In April 1986 Stan died at the age of 80. We all may come into the world with nothing, and we can certainly take nothing out. In leaving his name proudly emblazoned on a classic fleet now counted in their hundreds, Stan Robson was able to leave far more than anyone could hope to leave. If he needed more to ease his passing it was in the knowledge of the pleasure that he had given to countless people, myself included, who had followed his 'Border' fleet. That 1936 whim of copying that name on the Millican charabanc evolved into countless happy hours enjoyed by many, of 'Robson spotting', that was even a pleasure to the man himself.

In taking that decision to sell out as a going concern to the company of United Glass in 1980, he had at least given his offspring the chance to survive in the fickle service industry of road transport. Although the Nettleship influence had seen it transformed into a distribution company second to none, Robsons soon found itself a victim of circumstances that it had no control over.

It's a matter of historical record now that about April 1986, Distillers Co. Ltd were acquired by Guinness in a take-over bid championed by Chief Executive Ernest Saunders. The reverberations were to have a huge effect on many, and at the time of writing the circumstances surrounding the acquisition are currently being examined.

But back in '86, the result of the take-over was that United Glass Ltd and its division of Robsons Distribution Services were now 50% owned by Guinness. Having borrowed heavily to finance the take over, it became apparent Guinness would have to sell off many of the smaller facets of the Distillers organisation to repay some of the borrowing.

Pictured at Flitwick in March 1990, 'Border Bullet' is chassis number 252592 and came into service in November 1984. The vehicle was first run on a roaming itinerary as a 32 ton gross outfit with Roger Golding as its regular driver. With the addition of certain extra bolts into its fifth wheel coupling plates, the DAF was uprated for 38 tonnes work before being moved south to Bedfordshire.

Clearly displaying a 999 fleet number, 'Border Spitfire' was just in fact a Mercedes Benz demonstrator which came for short term appraisal. David Tinning is the Carlisle based driver seen behind the wheel. Other 'B' registered Mercedes which R.D.S. took use of were four 1625s worked out of Harlow, they being B649 BTU, B851 BLG, B863 BLG and B864 BLG.

(Below) 'Border Pegasus' is pictured loading paper reels at the Robson warehouse at Kirkbride. Even after the U.G take-over the site was still an important part in the Company distribution chain. Friday was its historically busiest day as men and vehicles amassed, loading up for the following week. This DAF 2800 was normally based at Glenrothes, it being new in November 1984 and having chassis number 257686.

After consultations with the other United Glass shareholder — Owens of Illinois — the decision was made to sell United Glass Ltd. An approach was received by a consortium to buy U.G. in total, but its two shareholders felt that a better price could be obtained if the divisions were sold off separately. These facts had to be kept very confidential, but in essence Robsons Distribution Services, in its own right, was up for sale. On a practical basis this made little difference to the day to day performance of Robsons. True, future developments of R.D.S. were put on hold, as Guinness didn't wish to authorise unnecessary investment, bearing in mind all the relevant circumstances.

Personnel who were on the move around that time saw George Flenley retire in 1986. George who had come from BRS to assist in the formation of the fledgeling Border Transport, grew with the Company to take over the post of Managing Director. Taking over the post of Commercial Director in the newly created R.D.S. he could naturally feel proud of the contribution he had made at Robsons. It seemed quite a while since February 1953 when he spent a lot of his time then running from one end of the garage in Metcalfe Street to the other end, to answer queries on both telephones. But the Flenley contribution wasn't finished quite yet as he was set to return to Robsons three years later, in the capacity of Business Development Consultant.

Herbert Nettleship was to take the post of Chairman whilst Simon Bellinger joined the Company in 1987 as Managing Director. He was to see the Company's title formalised into Robsons Distribution Services Ltd as it was bought by the Bunzl Group in January 1988.

The Group was to take its name from Moritz Bunzl who set up his haberdashery business in 1854. His three sons diversified into textile and paper waste trading, acquiring their first factory in Lower Austria. It was to be the paper industry that Bunzl specialised in, although in 1938 the family emigrated on the occupation of Austria.

Re-establishing their paper interests in the U.K. in 1940 it was the post-war growth in the market for filter tip cigarettes which prompted the huge success of the Group. As they grew they diversified into a wide range of other interests which as well as paper-related companies, also encompassed service and distribution concerns. They had bought York Trailers and the Neville body building concern, but in looking to expand their service and distribution division, they acquired Robsons Distribution Services Ltd.

Now, as a subsidiary to United Carriers International, Managing Director Bellinger decided to undertake some market research to establish how his Company of Robsons was being perceived. The results of being a solid, long established road haulier of high repute may have been foreseen, but it was also noted that the Company was not very well known in the South of England and it could really do with selling itself and its wide variety of services much more strongly.

Robsons had come a long way since 150+ vehicles were squeezed into their Carlisle base on a Friday night prior to drivers taking their weekend break. Their fleet of vehicles — some on dedicated contracts — was now based country-wide and as well as having a huge amount of strategic warehousing, they offered a high expertise in vehicle engineering, maintenance and service, plus the bonus of offering to train personnel as fork lift drivers.

The market research had felt the image needed to change to keep pace with what Robsons was all about and as fleet livery had so much influence on that conception, the colour scheme of the 200+ vehicles was put under the microscope. Numerous alternatives were tried to rejuvenate the standard cream and maroon livery, but in the end the difficult decision was made to change to that of the current predominance of white.

Incorporating the United Carriers logo chevrons, the name of Robsons appears strongly on the illuminated headboard, whilst the individual 'Border' name to the vehicle is still very much a strong part of the new look. Simon Bellinger said that he owed that particular decision to retain the Robson tradition, not least to Flitwick driver Claude. Very early in his Robson career, Simon had spoken to driver Claude who pointed out both his name and the fact that 'Border Claudius' was very much his own vehicle. Realising that having all your staff pulling for their company in a very positive manner was highly essential in this competitive field, encouraging pride of an individual driver in his own vehicle was a must so the 'Border' naming would stay on for ever.

Another important aspect that has seen recent change in the company, appertains to the traffic administration. Although Scotland has always had its own particular concentrated core of traffic peculiar to itself and their movements were co-ordinated from the Alloa depot, the rest of the

With both the name and the livery firmly established for the large fleet of R.D.S, the only key to where a vehicle was specifically based was to be given in the decal painted on the cab door centres. Befitting of its brand name,'Border Grouse' is based in the heart of whisky country at Alloa. Chassis number 1096701 was new into service during May 1985.

mainland traffic was centralised on a single office at St. Helens in July 1988.

Having the single office enhanced the working between regions. It also allowed Robsons to offer their major customers a delivery programme which sees them guarantee to deliver into a pre-determined window of 30 minutes. Since starting this service on 2nd January 1989, which affects 70-75% of the customer-destination or warehouse-destination full or part load type of movement, the service has achieved a 99.9% success rate. Even with the daily problems encountered when travelling by road, Robsons feel that it is only by giving their customer such a level of service that they can sustain their improvement in a highly competitive market place.

To co-ordinate all movements of the 200+ tractors and 500 trailers in and out of 19 depots/warehouses, the company requires the use of the high technology now available to the transport industry. It may not be long in fact when all the Robson road going fleet uses mobile communication.

Following on from that original market research, Robsons have extended into new ground with 350,000 sq.ft. of warehousing being opened at Sittingbourne, Wellsbourne, Southampton, Manchester and Newton-le-Willows. This took the total warehousing offered by Robsons to 1½ million square feet.

Other diversifications saw close co-operation with other U.C.I. sister companies which allowed for unaccompanied Robsons trailers to move via Calais into France and Europe. The same standard of half hour window deliveries was also available for traffic on this route, travelling in either direction.

B184 WBH, a Bedford KB41, was to be given the name 'Border Revival', it coming into service at Flitwick in October 1984. Being used as a first response breakdown vehicle, the pick up has covered a phenomenal distance in its stay. Fleet engineer Brian Geary reports it has given excellent service, with only its brakes requiring relining, a reflection of the vehicle's punishing timetable.

Stan Robson was to die in April 1986. One of his last photo calls about two years earlier, pictures him outside 'Wrayside', of course, wearing his cap. An injury to his hip meant that during his latter days he could only walk with the aid of a stick. He is pictured with two of his brothers who both served the Company well, they being Albert on the left, and Sid in the centre.

'Border Hamlet' and sister vehicle 'Ophelia' came as long term demonstrators and were in service until the end of 1988. Having the chassis number HG 45884, it is seen engaged providing propulsion to R.D.S. mechanic Jim Slater's son's pride and joy. The semi-trailer belongs to Lancer Boss and is normally used on fork lift delivery.

A new name for some Robson followers may be Iggesund Paperboard which was the Company which took over Thames Board in December 1987, which in turn was at the time part of the Unilever Group. MoDo is a compilation of two Swedish towns where Iggesund was formed, these being Mo and Domsjo. C197 PHH is ERF 'C' type formerly 'Border Cheviot'

Whilst the Company of Robsons worked both on their level of service and their image, the Bunzl Group were re-assessing their involvement in many aspects of business. This examination culminated in the decision to sell off United Carriers International, and on May 6th 1989, Robsons as an integral jewel in the crown of U.C.I., was part of a management buy out from the Bunzl Group.

With the control of the Company in the hands of its managers whilst the Banks and Financial Institutions who provided the capital look on, Robsons finds itself at an exciting point in its development. It is only natural that profit motivation now must come very high on the list of priorities for all employees. The one assured way to enhance this in the service industry of distribution is through quality of that service, an attitude that now must be the watchword of the Company.

How this is achieved means different things from different people. In welcoming George Flenley back as Business Development Consultant, Simon Bellinger was quoted as saying that Robsons commitment to quality of service was demonstrated by a combination of experience and pro-active marketing led development.

But it is the customer who must be the guide stick of a haulier's performance and endeavouring to keep that important person happy, Robsons have adopted two rules as a guide to customer relations. Rule 1 states "The customer is always right." Rule 2 states, "When the customer is wrong, refer to Rule 1."

There is no such thing as a Utopian state of road distribution but the nearest thing to achieving perfection is to

In the main the Robson drivers and their vehicles fall into three different groups. Apart from specific dedicated vehicles or local shunters, these are daymen, night men or roamers. 'Border Forth', one of the rivers batch of Scania 112s, is regularly used by day man Jimmy Hamilton who works out of the small base at Douglas Water. The 112 is chassis number 1107885 and was new in May 1986.

With the take-over of the Distillers Group and thus United Glass by Guinness, an early instruction to the transport arm of U.G. was to put a hold on the vehicle buying programme. This meant for over a year, that no new vehicles were purchased, and should have meant no 'D' registration vehicles appearing in the R.D.S. fleet list. 'Border Don' should have been registered C335 YLS when it was due into service during July 1986, but a slight hold up in registering it put the processing back a month and so the vehicle is unique being the sole 'D' registration on the list.

build up a very close relationship between yourself and your customer where the slightest difficulty is quickly sorted out.

In asking the thoughts from one customer of their feelings about Robsons it is perhaps fitting that the selection comes from their Cumbrian heartland. Thames Board Mills Ltd started production at Workington in 1967 converting timber into the basic packing material that eventually carries many of our well known household products. From those earliest days Robsons have given continued distribution of that Company's board and reel material. Twenty three years on Thames Board are now named Iggesund Paperboard (Workington) Ltd and whilst their favoured haulier has also changed ownership several times since Robsons Border Transport, the relationship between the two — customer and haulier — is still very close.

Perhaps Cumbrian people can be strange when they have such close affinity to people that they consider to be locals. Perhaps it is that reason why Iggesund feel that Robsons are almost part of their Workington company. Naturally market forces dictate that Robsons are not the only haulier out of their plant, but all Iggesund say is that if someone does a job for 23 years with all the competition available, draw your own conclusions as to why they are still very much a big part of the Workington process.

Explaining this type of affinity that Robsons have built up with their customers might be difficult, if not impossible. It is also difficult to explain the pleasurable feelings that many people have when they simply talk about Robsons or even see a 'Border' vehicle. Long may this pleasure continue.

With the announcement of the new 95, R.D.S. kept their allegiance with the DAF marque and bought large number of this new tractive unit. The 310bhp engine was specified as standard, this being the lesser powered of the two basic power pack options. The one drawback to the 95 in Chairman Herbert Nettleship's eyes is that its unladen weight is far too heavy. This trio of 95s is pictured in the Carlisle tractor park during a weekend in May 1989.

With total driver acceptance for the curtainsider bodywork on the semi-trailer, the step towards adopting this type of easily movable sides on the rigids was a natural one. 'Beaver' is rather an apt name for a Leyland DAF vehicle, the Carlisle based 1900 has Arnold Stobbard as its regular driver. Arnold beavers away each day delivering Castrol and BP oil based products around Cumbria going as far south as Barrow-in-Furness.

(Below) Coming new into service in early 1988, this batch of ERF E10 tractive units were supplied by Eden Commercial Services of Carlisle. Whilst nothing should be inferred by a name, the only vehicle not to last the passage of time is 'Border Poacher' which was written off after an accident, the R.D.S. driver being totally blameless. Whilst 'Rover' is naturally a roamer, the trio on right of shot are all worked hard on day and night trunking.

In late 1983 Robsons formalised their North Eastern operations by working out of the Elldis Transport yard at Newton Hall on the northern outskirts of Durham City. This arrangement continued until R.D.S. opened their own purpose built depot at Birtley which is closely adjacent to the A1(M) Durham motorway. 'Border Griffin' is a Birtley based vehicle with Kenny Whiteman being its regular day driver. The vehicle is seen waiting its night man Ernie Collard, fully loaded with paper pulp.

An entirely new facet of distribution was engaged on in early 1990 in work done on behalf of Johnson & Johnson. Based at Flitwick, G322 OAO along with two other MANs and two small VW vans, is used for lightweight delivery work around hospitals in London, East Anglia and the area of the South East. As yet, none of these vans have been named.

A new vehicle, a new livery, but the distinctive lines of a load of paper pulp illustrate an Iggesund Paperboard cargo that has been staple Robson work for more than 20 years. The new 'E' series ERF has Wilfe Harrison as its normal day driver and the maestro George Riley as its regular night man. George's normal journey is to Hilton Park to change over with another night man, northbound out of Flitwick.

Probably the most identifiable vehicle in the Robson fleet is 'Border Claudius' and as everyone, including the Managing Director, is aware, the name denotes the vehicle of regular driver Claude Barnes. Coming into service in January 1989, Claude ensured 'his' name was transferred from his old DAF 2800, B577 YGS, onto the L10 powered Roadtrain.

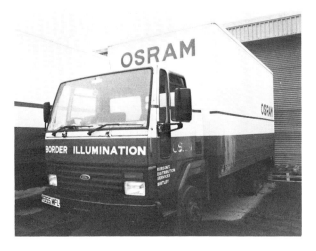

Robsons have regularly run their own vehicles in other people's colours with Carnation and Iggesund Paperboard (formerly Thames Board) being two obvious examples. But in the Birtley based 'Border Illumination', R.D.S. illustrate the offering of contract management to own account people, who may be in transport, but only as a necessity to deliver their own particular products.

When coupled to a matching curtainsider, the new livery on the R.D.S. flagships are a striking sight. The 95 is run both at 32 ton on four axles, whilst 'Minstrel' is seen at the highest possible weight band of 38 tonnes on five axles. The one obvious difference in livery content to R.D.S. followers is in the standardising of one single telephone number on the vehicles, which is the number of the R.D.S. Headquarters at Flitwick.

Fleet lists

F leet list gathering can be an emotive subject which always seems to revolve around discrepancies. I therefore categorically state that this is neither a comprehensive or even a totally correct listing of what Robsons have run throughout their history.

For ease of reference the fleet number is used to give consecutive reference. This form of numbering has been discontinued and although I was tempted to carry on giving details of extra vehicles currently in use, a fleet as large as Robsons is always on the change. Modern day followers of the Company will be able to update themselves via the Company's current spotters list together with their own observations.

The pre-nationalisation list has been compiled in the main by Robert Chicken consulting both photographs and accredited financial records of the Company. Where possible details of the vehicle have been confirmed by making reference to the rather sketchy records of the motor vehicle licensing department currently kept in store at Carlisle.

This method of cross reference has also been adopted

to check the earliest section of the post-nationalisation list but I feel sure there are many vehicles listed that may be questioned and again even more vehicles in use at the time which would fill some of the many gaps that are apparent. Any readers having such details are requested to contact the author who would greatly appreciate any up-date proffered.

Accrediting people in the compilation of this major list is very difficult. I feel sure that Malcolm Mortimer, Ray Jenkins and the master of lists, John Mollett will have had a great deal of input into its drawing up. Whilst they are the backbone to the list making, many others have fine tuned the list to clarify details and enhance its credibility. In this category I must include Geoff Milne as being of great help.

I have already mentioned in the text of the story the difficulties of recording a fleet which runs over the 1,000 mark. Due to the size of the task involved I hope readers bear with me, especially if I have quoted models as being slightly wrong. I feel sure there will be models of Foden quoted as an S39 that may well be an S34 or even an S36. It hasn't helped that Robsons didn't run any S21s - probably the most distinctive model that Foden ever produced - and only ran the sole S40, 'Border Eagle'.

But as well as being an historical record of what was run by Robsons, in the main it is an indulgence to the many of us who simply enjoy looking at the names of this fine 'Border' fleet.

ROBSONS HAULIERS (CARLISLE) LTD — Pre-nationalisation Fleet List

Fleet No.	Reg. No.	Type	Name	Driver
FD7	FTU 277	Foden OG 4 wheel platform	Prince	F Steel
FD8	HH 9783	Foden DG Chinese Six 6 wheel platform	Queen	R Mackenzie
FD9	GLG 483	Foden OG 4 wheel platform	Laddie	R T Mawson
FD10	ETU 771	Foden DG 4 wheel platform	Princess	L Rowlandson
		No information exists for fleet numbers 11, 12, 13 & 14		
BD15	CFS 261	Bristol 4 wheel platform	Rover	R Bell
ERFO16	DMA 722	ERF 4 wheel platform		
BD17		Bristol 4 wheel platform	Raider	G Trotter
AP18	JN 2854	Albion 4 wheel platform	Chief	
ERFO19	DMA 756	ERF 8 wheel platform	Baron	H Millican
AP20	HHT 417	Albion 4 wheel platform	Maiden	
FD21	BHH 542	Foden DG 8 wheel platform	King	C Steele
ERFO22	DMA 835	ERF 4 wheel platform	Roamer	E Bell
ERFO23	EAO 475	ERF 4 wheel platform	Soldier	T Pratt
ERFO24	CRM 365	ERF 4 wheel platform	Sailor	Newall
		No information exists for fleet number 25		
AP26	HH 9172	Albion 4 wheel platform	Duke	C Blair
BP27	GR 2327	Bedford 4 wheel van		
ERFO28	BHH 609	ERF 4 wheel tanker	Monarch	A Stevens
FD29	BHH 764	Foden DG 4 wheel platform	Empress	S Clifford
AD30	BHH 275	Albion 4 wheel platform	Knight	A Graham
ERFO31	EF 6888	ERF 4 wheel dropside	Emperor	T Leighton
AP32	HH 9754	Albion 4 wheel platform	Lassie	J Bell
BP33	GR 2596	Bedford 4 wheel van		
AP34	HH 9752	Albion 4 wheel platform	Spitfire	
BP35	BHH 438	Bedford		
AP36	AHH 337	Albion 4 wheel platform		
DP37	Not Reg.	Daimler 4 wheel drive recovery vehicle	Warrior	
BP38	BHH 904	Bedford artic	Duchess	D Coulthard
BP39	BHH 439	Bedford		
AP40	AHH 358	Albion 4 wheel platform	Hurricane	
FD41	FT 3724	Foden DG 4 wheel platform	Patrol	T Grieve
BP42	BHH 382	Bedford artic	Lady	J Straiton
AD43	AHH 362	Albion 4 wheel platform	Envoy	J H Bell
AD44	HH 9755	Albion 4 wheel platform	Ensign	Pantin
AD45	HH 8842	Albion 4 wheel platform	Beacon	R Hancock
AD46	HH 8871	Albion 4 wheel platform	Emblem	R Platt
BP47	BHH 440	Bedford 4 wheel van	Legion	F Calvert
FD48	CHH 385	Foden DG 8 wheel platform	Supreme	A Robson
FD49	BHH 516	Foden DG 6 wheel platform + drawbar	Majestic	Brown/Gibb
AD50	BHH 273	Albion 4 wheel platform	Clarion	W Douglas
AD51	BHH 272	Albion 4 wheel platform	Airman	G Douglas
AD52	AHH 359	Albion 4 wheel platform	Laird	
AD53	HH 9753	Albion 4 wheel platform	Viking	F Howes
AD54	AHH 999	Albion 4 wheel platform	Ranger	P Buntin
RD55	BHH 51	Reo 4 wheel platform	Clipper	R Parker
	FTU 94			J Atkinson
	CHH 515	Bedford 4 wheel van		
	CHH 535	Bedford artic		Jefferson
	CHH 574	Bedford		Skelton
	CHH 708	Foden DG 4 wheel platform	Renown	G Jackson
	CHH 865	Foden DG 4 wheel platform		Hancock
	CHH 916	Bedford-Scammell artic		
	BHH 212	Austin 4 wheel van		
	DHH 81	Foden 4 wheel platform		
	DHH 439	Bedford		

Regular driver's name stated where known

ROBSONS DISTRIBUTION SERVICES LTD   ROBSONS BORDER TRANSPORT LTD
Post Nationalisation fleet list — system now discontinued.

Fleet No.	Reg. No.	Type	Name
MTFP 1	XL 453	Model T Ford 4 wheeler	Veteran
		No information exists for fleet numbers 2, 3, 4, 5, 6, 7, 8, 9, 10 & 11	
FD 12	DHH 604	Foden 4 wheel platform	Prince
13	DHH 778	Bedford	Trooper
GD 14	DHH 813	Guy Otter 4 wheel churn carrier	Warrior
FD 15	DHH 804	Foden S18 4 wheel platform	Queen
		No information exists for fleet numbers 16 & 17	
18	CHH 44	Bedford 4 wheel platform	Comet
		No information exists for fleet numbers 19, 20, 21, 22, 23 & 24	
FD 25	EHH 542	Foden 4 wheel platform	Princess

Fleet No.	Reg.	Description	Name
		No information exists for fleet number 26	
FD 27	FHH 252	Foden 4 wheel platform	Baron
LD 28		Leyland Octopus 8 wheel platform	
FD 29	EHH 919	Foden 4 wheel platform	Regent
		No information exists for fleet numbers 30, 31, 32, 33, 34, 35, 36, 37, 38 & 39	
FD 40	EHH 334	Foden 8 wheel platform	Monitor
FD 41	GHH 590	Foden S18 4 wheel platform	Majestic
		No information exists for fleet numbers 42 & 43	
JD 44		Jensen 4 wheel platform	Laird
		No information exists for fleet number 45	
JD 46		Jensen 4 wheel platform	Count
AD 47	LAO 126	Albion 4 wheel platform	Laddie
TD 48	GHH 953	Ford Thames 4 wheel platform	Reliant
TD 49	GHH 954	Ford Thames 4 wheel platform	Defiant
AD 50	HHH 23	Albion Reiver 6 wheel platform	Monarch
FD 51	HHH 26	Foden S18 Chinese Six 6 wheeled platform	Duchess/Squire to 220
TD 52	HHH 24	Ford Thames 4 wheel platform	Gallant
TD 53	HHH 25	Ford Thames 4 wheel platform	Victor
TD 54	HHH 89	Ford Thames 4 wheel platform	Falcon
		No information exists for fleet number 55	
FD 56		Foden	Amazon
TD 57	HHH 424	Ford Thames 4 wheel van	Colleen
		No information exists for fleet number 58	
AD 59	BBV 772	Albion	Venture ex BRS 22C664
LD 60	FTY 555	Leyland Comet 4 wheel platform	Tudor
		No information exists for fleet number 61	
LD 62	KTB 921	Leyland Comet 4 wheel platform	Major
ERFO 63	BCB 742	ERF	Hunter ex BRS 22C675
		No information exists for fleet number 64	
JD 65	CSD 405	Jensen 4 wheel platform	Lancer
TD 66	HHH 611	Ford Thames 4 wheel platform	Valiant
TD 67	HHH 656	Ford Thames 4 wheel platform	Revenge
		No information exists for fleet numbers 68 & 69	
FD 70	LNE 49	Foden FG 8 wheel platform	Consort
FD 71	DBA 339	Foden DG 8 wheel platform	Viceroy
		No information exists for fleet number 72	
AD 73	HHH 832	Albion 4 wheel platform	Viscount
FD 74	BRJ 807	Foden	Emperor
FD 75	LMB 648	Foden	Premier
FD 76	ONB 299	Foden S18 8 wheel platform	Marquis
FD 77	EBN 244	Foden S18 8 wheel platform	Cavalier ex BRS 69C247
FD 78	NVU 532	Foden S18 8 wheel platform	King ex BRS 64C550
		No information exists for fleet numbers 79 & 80	
81	JOG 137	Bedford	Service
		No information exists for fleet numbers 82, 83 & 84	
AD 85	JHH 387	Albion Chieftain 4 wheel platform	Sailor
		No information exists for fleet numbers 86 & 87	
TD 88	JHH 507	Ford Thames 4 wheel platform	Rebel
89	BNL 233	Dodge	Nipper
90	EHH 519	Bedford 4 wheel platform	Swallow
		No information exists for fleet numbers 91 & 92	
LD 93	KTF 925	Leyland Octopus 8 wheel platform	Mariner
FD 94	JHH 800	Foden FE S18 4 wheel platform	Roamer
TD 95	JHH 865	Ford Thames 4 wheel platform	Swift
96	JXB 946	Bedford	Raven
97	CEO 815	Bedford	Maiden
		No information exists for fleet numbers 98 & 99	
FD 100	KHH 395	Foden S20 8 wheel platform	Century
		No information exists for fleet number 101	
FD 102	AJM 702	Foden DG 4 wheel platform	Pilot
SD 102	ESP 602	Scammell R8 8 wheel platform	Captain
		No information exists for fleet number 103	
FD 104	KAO 10	Foden OG4/6 4 wheel platform	Squire
AD 105	KHH 347	Albion Chieftain 4 wheel platform	Soldier
FD 106	DHH 872	Foden 4 wheel platform	Patrol/Laird
FD 107	KHH 446	Foden S20 4 wheel platform	Patriot
SD 108		Scammell R8 8 wheel platform	Patrol
SD 109	DGG 105	Scammell R8 8 wheel platform	Admiral ex BRS 63B404
TD 110	KHH 568	Ford 4 wheel van	Midget
SD 111	XS 5562	Scammell R8 8 wheel platform	Goliath
		No information exists for fleet number 112	
AD 113	FSG 837	Albion	Master
		No information exists for fleet number 114	
TD 115	KHH 766	Ford Thames Trader 4 wheel platform	Trader
FD 116	GHH 137	Foden FE 4 wheel platform Bowyer cab	Raider
TD 117	KHH 767	Ford Thames Trader 4 wheel platform	Rover
TD 118	LHH 79	Ford Thames Trader 4 wheel platform	Winner
TD 119	LHH 262	Ford Thames Trader 4 wheel platform	Lancer
120	MXX 743	Bedford	Dragon
TD 121	LHH 314	Ford Thames Trader - County 6 wheel platform	Consul
		No information exists for fleet number 122	
FD 123	SAO 160	Ford Thames 4 wheel platform	Tribute
		No information exists for fleet number 124	
TD 125	LHH 502	Ford Thames Trader 4 wheel platform	Rambler
TD 126	LHH 550	Ford Thames Trader Tractor	Pullman
FD 127	LHH 572	Foden S20 8 wheel platform dropside	Queen
FD 128	LHH 608	Foden S20 8 wheel platform	Senior
AD 129	JSM 262	Albion Chieftain 4 wheel platform	Yeoman
FD 130	LHH 770	Foden S20 8 wheel platform	Empress
FD 131	LHH 777	Ford Thames Trader	Trojan
		No information exists for fleet number 132	
TD 133	GHH 788	Ford Thames 4 wheel platform	Hornet
AD 134	NAO 324	Albion Chieftain 4 wheel platform	Ensign
FD 135	HRM 291	Foden (ex W.D.)	Retriever
		No information exists for fleet number 136	
FD 137	SUM 53	Foden S18 8 wheel platform	Legion
FD 138	SUB 713	Foden S18 8 wheel platform	Sceptre
FD 139	SUB 719	Foden S18 8 wheel platform	Hunter
SD 140	MMH 10	Scammell R8 8 wheel platform	Patrol
TD 141	MHH 757	Ford Thames Trader 4 wheel platform	Pioneer
142	CHH 889	Bedford	Bantam
TD 143	MHH 849	Ford Thames Trader Tractor	Cadet
TD 144	MHH 950	Ford Thames Trader	Service
FD 145	NNE 790	Foden S18 8 wheel platform/mobile crane	Courier/Samson
FD 146	NNE 648	Foden S18 8 wheel platform	Admiral
FD 147	NHH 54	Foden S20 8 wheel platform	Patrol
AD 148	KRM 289	Albion 4 wheel van	Prince
TD 149	NHH 202	Ford Thames Trader - County 6 wheel platform	Prefect
150	BJM 537	ERF KV 4 wheel platform	Rocket
TD 151	NHH 336	Ford Thames Trader 4 wheel platform	Rajah/Venture
TD 152	VAO 32	Ford Thames Trader 4 wheel platform	Sultan
AD 153	GXD 278	Albion Chieftain 4 wheel flat churn carrier	Clipper
AD 154	BBV 10	Albion Chieftain 4 wheel flat churn carrier	Count
FD 155	NHH 600	Foden S20 8 wheel platform	Supreme
TD 156	NHH 761	Ford Thames Trader 4 wheel platform	Hussar
TD 157	NHH 925	Ford Thames Trader 4 wheel platform	Gunner
FD 158	NHH 965	Foden S20 8 wheel platform	Emperor
TD 159	OHH 39	Ford Thames Trader 4 wheel van	Viking
TD 160	DEC 786	Ford Thames Trader	Mayor
FD 161	OHH 494	Foden S20 8 wheeler/4 wheel tractor	Knight/Tester
AD 162	VAO 723	Albion Caledonian 8 wheel platform	Provost
TD 163	URM 577	Ford Thames Trader 4 wheel platform	Marine
TD 164	OHH 622	Ford Thames Trader 4 wheel platform	Skipper
		No information exists for fleet number 165	
TD 166	MHH 62	Ford Thames Trader 4 wheel platform	Frigate
LD 167	MJR 102	Leyland 4 wheel platform	Trooper
TD 168	OHH 820	Ford Thames Trader 4 wheel platform	Advance
FD 169	PHH 71	Foden S20 4 wheel tractor	Ranger
FD 170	PHH 72	Foden S20 8 wheel platform	Premier
TD 171	PHH 112	Ford Thames Trader Tractor	Colleen
TD 172	PHH 224	Foden FE 4 wheel tractor - Bowyer Cab	Laddie
TD 173	PHH 225	Ford Thames Trader 4 wheel platform	Senator
TD 174	PHH 325	Ford Thames Trader 4 wheel platform	Sheriff
TD 175	LHH 917	Ford Thames Trader 4 wheel platform	Gallant
TD 176	MHH 198	Ford Thames Trader 4 wheel platform	Victor
TD 177	MHH 199	Ford Thames Trader 4 wheel platform	Falcon
TD 178	MHH 197	Ford Thames Trader 4 wheel platform	Deputy
TD 179	LHH 915	Ford Thames Trader 4 wheel platform	Escort
TD 180	LHH 916	Ford Thames Trader 4 wheel platform	Marshal
TD 181	PHH 786	Ford Thames Trader 4 wheel platform	Panther
FD 182	PHH 954	Foden S20 8 wheel platform dropside	Cavalier
TP 183	PHH 919	Ford Thames 7cwt van	Valet
AD 184	RHH 413	Albion Reiver 6 wheel platform	Reiver
AD 185	LAO 130	Albion Chieftain 4 wheel platform	Tudor
AD 186	NRM 863	Albion Chieftain 4 wheel platform	Tutor

FD 187	RHH 516	Foden S20 8 wheel platform	Prince
CD 188	HAO 79	Coles 4 wheel mobile crane	Goliath
TD 189	RHH 662	Ford Thames Trader 4 wheel platform	Comet
TD 190	RHH 912	Ford Thames Trader 4 wheel platform	Captain
FD 191	RHH 885	Foden S20 8 wheel platform dropside	Unicorn
TD 192	RHH 913	Ford Thames Trader 4 wheel platform	Sabre
		No information exists for fleet numbers 193 & 194	
TD 195	SHH 38	Ford Thames Trader 4 wheel platform	Cruiser
TD 196	SHH 57	Ford Thames Trader 4 wheel platform	Husky
TD 197	MNL 839	Ford Thames Trader 4 wheel platform	Hawk
AD 198	SHH 284	Albion Reiver 6 wheel platform	Lassie
TD 199	NHH 336	Ford Thames Trader 4 wheel platform	Venture
199	SHH 282	Ford Thames Trader 4 wheel flat dropside	Pennant To 213
AD 200	SHH 283	Albion Reiver 6 wheel platform	Renown
FD 201	SHH 285	Foden S20 8 wheel platform dropside	Viceroy
AD 202	SHH 366	Albion Reiver 6 wheel platform dropside	Laird
AD 203	SHH 460	Albion Reiver 6 wheel platform	Sherpa
FD 204	SHH 606	Foden S20 8 wheel platform dropside	Roamer
AD 205	SHH 652	Albion Reiver 6 wheel platform	Herald
AD 206	SHH 651	Albion Reiver 6 wheel platform	Phantom
FD 207	SHH 676	Foden S20 8 wheel platform	King
		No information exists for fleet numbers 208 & 209	
TD 210	NHH 761	Ford Thames Trader 4 wheel platform	Rajah
TD 211	SHH 908	Ford Thames Trader 4 wheel platform	Rocket
		No information exists for fleet number 212	
TD 213	SHH 282	Ford Thames Trader 4 wheel dropside	Pennant Was 199
TD 214	THH 456	Ford Thames Trader - County 6 wheel platform	Classic
214	THH 314	Ford Thames Trader 4 wheel platform	Spartan
FD 215	THH 484	Foden S20 8 wheel platform dropside	Monarch
TD 216	THH 591	Ford Thames Trader 4 wheel platform	Sputnick
TD 217	THH 663	Ford Thames Trader 4 wheel platform	Jester
TD 218	THH 970	Ford Thames Trader 4 wheel platform	Drifter
FD 219	UHH 11	Foden S20 8 wheel platform dropside	Bulwark
FD 220	HHH 26	Foden S18 Chinese 6 platform	Squire Was 51
TD 221	UHH 130	Ford Thames Trader 4 wheel platform 75	Bailiff
AD 222	ASW 17	Albion Chieftain 4 wheel platform	Duke
TD 223	UHH 155	Ford Thames Trader 4 wheel platform 75	Sentry
TD 224	UHH 188	Ford Thames Trader Tractor	Chief
TD 225	UHH 349	Ford Thames Trader platform	Escort
225	FEC 35	Ford Thames Trader 4 wheel platform	Cadet
FD 226	UHH 348	Foden S20 8 wheel platform	Warrior
FD 227	UHH 409	Foden S20 8 wheel platform	Dandy
FD 228	UHH 430	Foden S20 8 wheel platform dropside	Trident
FD 229	UHH 460	Foden S20 8 wheel platform	Bounty
FD 230	UHH 284	Foden S20 8 wheel platform	Dauphin
FD 231	UHH 481	Foden S20 8 wheel platform dropside	Consort
FD 232	UHH 497	Foden S20 8 wheel platform dropside	Meteor
TD 233	UHH 570	Ford Thames Trader platform	Capri
TD 234	UHH 550	Foden S20 8 wheel platform dropside	Duchess
FD 235	UHH 603	Foden S20 8 wheel platform	Pioneer
FD 236	UHH 659	Foden S20 8 wheel platform dropside	Courier
AD 237	UHH 738	Albion Reiver 6 wheel platform	Stuart
FD 238	UHH 774	Foden S20 8 wheel platform	Raider
238	UHH 724	Foden S20 8 wheel platform dropside	Warden
TD 239	VHH 18	Ford Thames Trader 4 wheel platform 75	Student
AD 240	VHH 113	Albion Chieftain 4 wheel platform	Provost
TD 241	VHH 420	Ford Thames Trader 4 wheel platform 75	Batman
FD 242	VHH 484	Foden S20 8 wheel platform	Baron
AD 243	VHH 524	Albion Chieftain 'Super 6' 4 wheel platform	Piper
TD 244	VHH 730	Ford Thames Trader 4 wheel platform	Popular
TD 245	VHH 914	Ford Thames Trader 4 wheel platform 75	Guide
AD 246	OAO 427	Albion Chieftain 4 wheel platform	Yeoman
TD 247	WHH 34	Ford Thames Trader 4 wheel platform Mk II	Shiekh
FD 248	WHH 88	Foden platform	Rambler
TD 249	WHH 226	Ford Thames Trader platform	Regent
TD 250	WHH 279	Ford Thames Trader Tractor Mk II	Dragon
TD 251	WHH 299	Ford Thames Trader platform	Pilot
FD 252	WHH 367	Foden S20 8 wheel platform dropside	Princess
AD 253	WHH 632	Albion Reiver 6 wheel platform dropside	Telstar
TD 254	WHH 781	Ford Thames Trader Tractor Mk II	Leader
TD 255	WHH 836	Ford Thames Trader	Legend To 370
AD 256	WHH 835	Albion Tractor	Polaris
TD 257	WHH 907	Ford Thames Trader Tractor Mk II	Rebel
TD 258	WHH 919	Ford Thames Trader Tractor Mk II	Maestro
TD 259	WHH 948	Ford Thames Trader Tractor	Squire
TD 260	XHH 42	Ford Thames Trader Tractor	Legion
AD 261	XHH 31	Albion Reiver 6 wheel platform	Hunter
TD 262	RHH 913	Ford Thames Trader 4 wheel platform	Sabre
		No information exists for fleet number 263	
FD 264	XHH 407	Foden S34 Tractor	Pullman
TD 265	468 DTN	Ford Thames Trader 4 wheel platform	Titan
TD 266	SHH 281	Ford Thames Trader	Caddy
AD 267	NHH 708	Albion Chieftain 4 wheel platform	Tourist
268	KBR 983	Dodge-Primrose conversion 6 wheel platform	Agent
269	YAO 776	ERF	Scout
270	RHH 846	Commer	Canuk
TD 271	XHH 713	Ford Thames Trader 4 wheel van	Page
TD 272	XHH 884	Ford Thames Trader Tractor Mk II	Safari
TD 273	XHH 852	Ford Thames Trader 4 wheel platform	Host
FD 274	XHH 864	Foden S34 Tractor	Marquis
275	XHH 871	Commer	Skipper
TD 276	YHH 52	Ford Thames Trader 4 wheel platform Mk II	Prefect
TD 277	YHH 182	Ford Thames Trader 4 wheel platform	Condor
TD 278	NCK 286	Ford Thames Trader 4 wheel tipper	Tipster
TD 279	YHH 415	Ford Thames Trader 4 wheel platform	Trader
FD 280	YHH 473	Foden S34 Tractor	Wanderer
TD 281	YHH 507	Ford Thames Trader 4 wheel platform	Sultan
FD 282	CEB 983	Foden Tractor	Python
		No information exists for fleet number 283	
TD 284	AHH 2B	Ford Thames Trader 4 wheel platform	Beatle
FD 285	AHH 1B	Foden S34 Tractor	Hostess
AD 286	AHH 224B	Albion platform	Panther
TD 287	AHH 286B	Ford Thames Trader 4 wheel platform	Umpire
TD 288	AHH 291B	Ford Thames Trader Tractor Mk II	Maiden
AD 289	AHH 310B	Albion platform	Crofter
TD 290	AHH 398B	Ford Thames Trader Tractor	Deputy
TD 291	AHH 391B	Ford Thames Trader Tractor	Tribute
TD 292	AHH 421B	Ford Thames Trader Tractor Mk II	Comet
TD 293	AHH 441B	Ford Thames Trader	Ensign
TD 294	AHH 504B	Ford Thames Trader Tractor	Tattoo
TD 295	AHH 585B	Ford Thames Trader Tractor	Falcon
TD 296	AHH 650B	Ford Thames Trader	Wizard
FD 297	AHH 594B	Foden S34 Tractor	Countess
TD 298	AHH 927B	Ford Thames Trader 4 wheel platform	Gurkha
TD 299	BHH 111B	Ford Thames Trader platform	Tutor
TD 300	BHH 110B	Ford Thames Trader	Swift
TD 301	BHH 112B	Ford Thames Trader 4 wheel platform	Arrow
TD 302	BHH 113B	Ford Thames Trader	Lancer
TD 303	BHH 394B	Ford Thames Trader platform	Rover
TD 304	BHH 410B	Ford Thames Trader 4 wheel platform	Frigate
AD 305	BHH 446B	Albion Tractor	Clansman
FD 306	BHH 563B	Foden Tractor	Patriot
FD 307	BHH 902B	Foden Tractor	Eskimo
TD 308	BHH 962B	Ford Thames Trader Tractor	Athlete
TD 309	BHH 942B	Ford Thames Trader Tractor	Major
TD 310	388 JWC	Ford Thames Trader 4 wheel platform	Venture
TD 311	CHH 180B	Ford Thames Trader 4 wheel platform	Agent
311	CHH 228B	Foden S39 Tractor	Majestic
FD 312	CHH 238B	Foden Tractor	Emblem
FD 313	CHH 505B	Ford Thames Trader platform	Trunker
FD 314	PTB 281	Foden S18 Tractor	Shunter
TD 315	CHH 588C	Ford Thames Trader Tractor	Eagle
TD 316	CHH 546C	Ford Thames Trader Tractor	Colleen
TD 317	CHH 566C	Ford Thames Trader 4 wheel platform	Raven
TD 318	CHH 594C	Ford Thames Trader 4 wheel platform	Hawk
AD 319	CHH 609C	Albion Reiver 6 wheel platform	Scottie
FD 320	EHH 624C	Foden Tractor	Sceptre
TD 321	CHH 722C	Ford Thames Trader Tractor	Titan
TD 322	JTW 421C	Ford Tractor	Explorer
		No information exists for fleet number 323	
TD 324	761 ARM	Ford Tipper	Tipster
		No information exists for fleet number 325	
AD 326	DHH 52C	Albion platform	Kiltie

Fleet	Reg	Description	Name
AD 327	DHH 225C	Albion platform	Kinsman
TD 328	DHH 510C	Ford Thames Trader Tractor	Compere
AD 329	DHH 566C	Albion Reiver 6 wheel platform	Renown
TD 330	EHH 563C	Ford	Collie
AD 331	DHH 623C	Albion Tractor	Laddie
FD 332	DHH 602C	Foden Tractor	Duke
AD 333	DHH 939C	Albion Tractor	Chieftain
TD 334	DHH 969C	Ford platform	Marine
No information exists for fleet number 335			
TD 336	EHH 63C	Ford Tractor	Beagle
FD 337	EHH 153C	Foden Tractor	Leader
FD 338	EHH 167C	Foden S34 Tractor	Symbol
FD 339	EHH 311C	Foden S34 Tractor	Senior
TD 340	UHH 360	Ford	Caddy
FD 341	EHH 347C	Ford 'D' Tractor	Legend
FD 342	EHH 482C	Ford 'D' Tractor	Custom
FD 343	EHH 490C	Foden S39 Tractor	Patrol
TD 344	EHH 557C	Ford Thames Trader platform	Dalek
AD 345	EHH 586C	Albion Tractor	Claymore
FD 346	EHH 630C	Foden Tractor	Emperor
FD 347	EHH 724C	Ford 'D' Tractor	Squire
No information exists for fleet number 348			
349	EHH 851C	Ford	Sentry
FD 350	EHH 949C	Foden Tractor	Sentinel
No information exists for fleet number 351			
FD 352	FHH 126D	Ford 'D' Tractor	Searcher
FD 353	FHH 193D	Ford 'D' 4 wheel platform	Archer
FD 354	FHH 221D	Foden S39 Tractor	Queen
FD 355	FHH 303D	Ford 'D' 4 wheel platform	Author
FD 356	FHH 299D	Ford 'D' 4 wheel platform	Tornado
FD 357	FHH 308D	Ford 'D' 4 wheel platform	Typhoon
AD 358	FHH 753D	Albion platform	Tartan
FD 359	FHH 810D	Ford 'D' 4 wheel platform	Marathon
FD 360	HNO 910B	Ford 'D' Tractor	Hero
AD 361	GHH 75D	Albion platform	Dirk
FD 362	GHH 640D	Foden S36 Tractor	Empress
AD 363	GHH 665D	Albion platform	Phantom
FD 364	GHH 719D	Ford 'D' Tractor	Gallant
FD 365	GHH 791D	Ford 'D' Tractor	Sabre
FD 366	GHH 815D	Ford 'D' Tractor	Orderly
FD 367	HHH 33D	Ford 'D' 4 wheel platform	Airman
FD 368	HHH 144D	Foden Tractor	Usher
FD 369	HHH 238D	Foden Tractor	Supreme
FD 370	WHH 836	Ford Thames Trader	Titan Was 255
FD 371	HHH 366D	Foden S39 Tractor	Concord
No information exists for fleet number 372			
FD 373	HHH 395D	Ford 'D' Tractor	Corsair
FD 374	HHH 387D	Ford 'D' Tractor	Drummer
AD 375	HHH 450D	Albion platform	Polaris
FD 376	HHH 501D	Foden Tractor	Governor
FD 377	HHH 586E	Foden S39 Tractor	Oscar
FD 378	HHH 685E	Ford 'D' Tractor	Commando
FD 379	HHH 955E	Foden S39 Tractor	Cavalier
379	CHH 483B	Ford Van	Riddler
FD 380	JHH 204E	Foden S39 Tractor	Viceroy
FD 381	JHH 216E	Ford 'D' Tractor	Regent
FD 382	PHH 427	Ford 4 wheel van	Valet
No information exists for fleet number 383			
FD 384	JHH 367E	Foden S39 Tractor	Captain
FD 385	JHH 725E	Foden S39 Tractor	Roamer
FD 386	JHH 996E	Foden S39 Tractor	King
FD 387	MTW 822C	Ford Tractor	Select
FD 388	KHH 387F	Foden Tractor	Bulwark
FD 389	KHH 432F	Ford 'D' Tractor	Lancer
FD 390	KHH 431F	Ford 'D' Tractor	Tutor
FD 391	KHH 434F	Ford 'D' Tractor	Arrow
FD 392	KHH 433F	Ford 'D' Tractor	Terrier
FD 393	KHH 463F	Foden Tractor	Dauphin
394	PAO 292	Land Rover	Swift
FD 395	KHH 668F	Foden S39 Tractor	Warrior
FD 396	KHH 894F	Foden Tractor	Express
FD 397	KHH 911F	Ford 'D' Tractor	Wizard
AD 398	LHH 68F	Albion Reiver 6 wheel platform	Highlander
FD 399	LHH 48F	Foden S36 Tractor	Dandy
FD 400	LHH 146F	Ford 'D' 4 wheel platform	Gurkha
FD 401	KHH 773F	Ford 'D' Tractor	Pride
FD 402	LHH 273F	Ford 'D' Tractor	Lotus
FD 403	LHH 624F	Foden S39 Tractor	Buccaneer
FD 404	LHH 624F	Ford 'D' 4 wheel platform	Collie
FD 405	LHH 625F	Foden S39 Tractor	Consort
No information exists for fleet number 406			
FD 407	LHH 768F	Ford 'D' Tractor	Viking
FD 408	LHH 811F	Foden S39 Tractor	Meteor
AD 409	MHH 36F	Albion Reiver 6 wheel platform	Bandit
FD 410	MHH 32F	Ford 'D' Tractor	Gypsy
FD 411	MHH 113F	Ford 'D' Tractor	Renegade
FD 412	MHH 228F	Ford 'D' 4 wheel platform	Brigand
FD 413	MHH 216F	Foden S39 Tractor	Rover
414	MHH 301F	Ford 4 wheel van	Rescue
FD 415	MHH 515F	Foden S39 Tractor	Duchess
AD 416	MHH 705F	Albion Reiver 6 wheel platform	Gillie
FD 417	MHH 863F	Foden S39 Tractor	Courier
FD 418	NHH 318G	Foden S39 Tractor	Warden
FD 419	NHH 351G	Foden S39 Tractor	Baron
419	EHH 763C	Ford 'D' Tractor	Raider
No information exists for fleet number 420			
FD 421	NHH 592G	Foden S39 Tractor	Rambler
FD 422	NHH 892G	Ford 'D' Tractor	Yeoman
FD 423	NHH 895G	Foden S39 Tractor	Bounty
FD 424	OHH 161G	Foden S39 Tractor	Guardsman
FD 425	OHH 109G	Ford 'D' Tractor	Angler
FD 426	OHH 159G	Foden S39 Tractor	Pioneer
FD 427	OHH 145G	Foden S39 Tractor	Princess
FD 428	OHH 156G	Foden S39 Tractor	Dragoon
FD 429	OHH 192G	Ford 'D' Tractor	Spaceman
FD 430	OHH 184G	Ford 'D' Tractor	Drifter
FD 431	OHH 208G	Ford 'D' Tractor	Apollo
FD 432	NHH 891G	Ford 'D' Tractor	Gazelle
FD 433	NHH 244G	Ford 'D' Tractor	Escort
No information exists for fleet numbers 434 & 435			
FD 436	OHH 424G	Ford 'D' Tractor	Beaver
FD 437	OHH 375G	Foden S39 Tractor	Cosmos
FD 438	OHH 526G	Foden S39 Tractor	Hurricane
FD 439	OHH 565G	Foden S39 Tractor	Jobber
FD 440	OHH 576G	Ford 'D' Tractor	Sailor
FD 441	OHH 891G	Foden S39 Tractor	Panther
FD 442	PHH 14G	Ford 'D' 4 wheel platform	Hunter
FD 443	PHH 83G	Foden S39 Tractor	Marshall
FD 444	PHH 128G	Ford 'D' Tractor	Clipper
FD 445	PHH 315G	Foden S39 Tractor	Matador
FD 446	PHH 346G	Ford 'D' Tractor	Toreador
FD 447	PHH 424G	Ford 'D' Tractor	Picador
FD 448	PHH 616G	Foden S39 Tractor	Tourist
FD 449	PHH 651G	Foden S39 Tractor	Patriot
FD 450	PHH 672G	Ford 'D' 4 wheel platform	Primate
FD 451	PHH 807H	Foden S39 Tractor	Marquis
FD 452	PHH 817H	Ford 'D' 4 wheel platform	Ballad
FD 453	PHH 814H	Foden S39 Tractor	Wanderer
FD 454	PHH 979H	Ford 'D' 4 wheel platform	Porter
FD 455	PHH 985H	Foden S39 Tractor	Gambler
AD 456	RHH 188H	Albion Tractor	Renown
AD 457	RHH 189H	Albion Tractor	Pedlar
FD 458	RHH 201H	Foden S39 Tractor	Hussar
FD 459	RHH 372H	Ford 'D' Tractor	Deputy
FD 460	RHH 405H	Foden S39 Tractor	Tribute
FD 461	RHH 531H	Ford 'D' 4 wheel platform	Cossack
FD 462	RHH 296H	Ford 'D' Tractor	Colonel
FD 463	RHH 588H	Foden S39 Tractor	Monarch
FD 464	RHH 691H	Ford 'D' Tractor	Cyclone
FD 465	RHH 697H	Foden S39 Tractor	Tycoon
FD 466	RHH 798H	Ford 4 wheel van	Bronco
FD 467	RHH 876H	Ford 'D' 4 wheel van	Athlete
FD 468	RHH 910H	Ford 'D' Tractor	Bailiff
FD 469	RHH 912H	Ford 'D' Tractor	Poacher
FD 470	SHH 141H	Ford 'D' 4 wheel platform	Colleen
FD 471	RHH 936H	Ford 'D' Tractor	Puffin
FD 472	RHH 933H	Ford 'D' Tractor	Kestrel
FD 473	RHH 939H	Ford 'D' Tractor	Falcon

Fleet No.	Reg.	Type	Name
FD 474	SHH 152H	Foden S39 Tractor	Volunteer
FD 475	SHH 127H	Ford 'D' Tractor	Recruit
FD 476	SHH 287H	Foden S39 Tractor	Crusader
FD 477	SHH 392H	Ford 'D' Tractor	Chariot
FD 478	SHH 471H	Foden S39 Tractor	Countess
FD 479	MDJ 668E	Ford Transit 4 wheel van	Transit
FD 480	SHH 611H	Ford 'D' Tractor	Dolphin
FD 481	SHH 589H	Foden S39 Tractor	Avenger
FD 482	SHH 675H	Ford 'D' 4 wheel platform	Artisan
482	SHH 756H	Ford 'D' Tractor	Caddie
FD 483	SHH 757H	Ford 'D' Tractor	Major
FD 484	SHH 949H	Foden S39 Tractor	Eskimo
AD 485	THH 94H	Albion Tractor	Duke
FD 486	THH 182H	Foden S39 Tractor	Aquarius
FD 487	THH 346H	Ford 'D' 4 wheel platform	Select
FD 488	THH 374H	Ford 'D' 4 wheel platform	Prefect
No information exists for fleet number 489			
FD 490	THH 564H	Foden S39 Tractor	Gladiator
FD 491	THH 597H	Ford 'D' 4 wheel platform	Sultan
FD 492	THH 626H	Foden S39 Tractor	Leader
FD 493	THH 802J	Foden S39 Tractor	Premier
FD 494	UHH 37J	Foden S39 Tractor	Ranger
FD 495	UHH 51J	Foden S39 Tractor	Invader
495	AMB 548F	Ford Transit 4 wheel van	Valet
FD 496	UHH 193J	Foden S39 Tractor	Royalist
FD 497	UHH 276J	Foden S39 Tractor	Pilgrim
497	FHH 787D	Foden S39 Tractor	Emperor
No information exists for fleet number 498			
FD 499	ORM 532F	Ford 'D' Tractor	Badger
FD 500	GHH 369D	Foden S39 Tractor	Viscount
FD 501	UHH 703J	Foden S39 Tractor	Grenadier
FD 502	UHH 838J	Foden S39 Tractor	Professor
No information exists for fleet number 503			
FD 504	VHH 36J	Foden S39 Tractor	Fusilier
FD 505	VHH 23J	Ford 'D' 4 wheel platform	Farrier
FD 506	UHH 959J	Ford 'D' Tractor	Harrier
FD 507	VHH 173J	Foden S39 Tractor	Senior
FD 508	VHH 428J	Foden S39 Tractor	Executive
FD 509	VHH 631J	Foden S39 Tractor	Adonis
FD 510	UHH 655J	Foden S39 Tractor	Tristar
FD 511	VHH 886J	Foden S39 Tractor	Fisher
FD 512	WHH 234J	Foden S39 Tractor	Phantom
FD 513	WHH 241J	Foden S39 Tractor	Banshee
FD 514	WHH 644K	Ford 'D' Tractor	Rocket
FD 515	WHH 665K	Ford 'D' Tractor	Tempest
FD 516	WHH 651K	Foden S39 Tractor	Venture
AD 517	WHH 750K	Albion Tractor	Crofter
AD 518	WHH 755K	Albion Tractor	Reiver
FD 519	WHH 887K	Ford 'D' Tractor	Fireman
AD 520	WHH 876K	Albion Tractor	Claymore
FD 521	WHH 889K	Foden S39 Tractor	Valiant
FD 522	WHH 955K	Foden S39 Tractor	Guardian
FD 523	XHH 42K	Foden S39 Tractor	Victor
AD 524	XHH 63K	Albion Tractor	Outlaw
AD 525	XHH 156K	Albion Tractor	Kiltie
FD 526	XHH 389K	Ford 'D' Tractor	Mustang
FD 527	XHH 357K	Foden S39 Tractor	Regal
FD 528	XHH 425K	Ford 'D' Tractor	Maverick
No information exists for fleet number 529 & 530			
FD 531	XHH 616K	Foden S39 Tractor	Courage
FD 532	XHH 648K	Foden S39 Tractor	Patrol
FD 533	XHH 836K	Foden S39 Tractor	Destiny
FD 534	XHH 809K	Ford 'D' Tractor	Student
FD 535	XHH 874K	Ford 'D' Tractor	Minstrel
FD 536	YHH 133K	Ford 'D' Tractor	Mariner
FD 537	YHH 43K	Foden S39 Tractor	Conquest
FD 538	YHH 498K	Foden S39 Tractor	Vampire
FD 539	YHH 607K	Foden S39 Tractor	Cavalier
FD 540	AHH 21K	Foden S39 Tractor	Viscount
FD 541	AHH 77K	Foden S39 Tractor	Prince
FD 542	AHH 330K	Foden S39 Tractor	Defiant
FD 543	AHH 388K	Foden S39 Tractor	Emperor
FD 544	AHH 605K	Ford 'D' Tractor	Raider
FD 545	AHH 680K	Ford 'D' Tractor	Yeoman
FD 546	TMD 426F	Ford 'D' 4 wheel platform	Merchant
FD 547	AHH 903L	Foden S39 Tractor	Sherpa
FD 548	BHH 111L	Foden S39 Tractor	Cruiser
FD 549	BHH 281L	Foden S39 Tractor	Unicorn
FD 550	BHH 390L	Foden S40 Tractor	Castle/Eagle
FD 551	BHH 422L	Foden S39 Tractor	Cardinal
FD 552	BHH 511L	Foden S39 Tractor	Neptune
FD 553	BHH 517L	Ford 'D' Tractor	Pioneer
553	BHH 783L	Ford 'D' Tractor	Herald
FD 554	BHH 774L	Ford 'D' 4 wheel platform	Brigand
FD 555	BHH 937L	Ford 'D' Tractor	Hadrian
FD 556	CHH 601L	Foden S39 Tractor	Trident
FD 557	CHH 599L	Foden Tractor	Concorde
FD 558	DHH 870L	Foden S80 Tractor	Europa
FD 559	EHH 340L	Foden S80 Tractor	Supreme
FD 560	OHH 364M	Foden S80 Tractor	Reliant
LD 561	RTJ 711M	Leyland Clydesdale Tractor	Clipper
FD 562	OHH 788M	Ford 'D' 4 wheel van	Hornet
FD 563	OHH 992M	Foden S80 Tractor	Merlin
FD 564	PHH 1M	Foden S80 Tractor	Queen
FD 565	PHH 144M	Foden S80 Tractor	Vulcan
FD 566	LHD 926L	Ford 4 wheel van	Transit
FD 567	PHH 307M	Ford 'D' Tractor	Lancer
FD 568	PHH 402M	Foden S80 Tractor (Carnation Livery)	
FD 569	PHH 324M	Foden S80 Tractor (Carnation Livery)	
FD 570	PHH 412M	Foden Tractor	Drifter
LD 571	RHH 40M	Leyland Clydesdale 4 wheel platform	Terrier
LD 572	RHH 129M	Leyland Clydesdale Tractor	Beaver
FD 573	RHH 641N	Foden S80 Tractor	Cumbrian
LD 574	RHH 690N	Leyland Clydesdale Tractor	Trader
FD 575	GAO 273N	Foden S80 Tractor	Amazon
FD 576	GAO 422N	Ford 'D' 4 wheel van	Arrow
LD 577	GAO 388N	Leyland Clydesdale Tractor	Chieftain
FD 577	HHH 751N	Foden S80 Tractor	Renown
No information exists for fleet number 578			
FD 579	JHH 474N	Foden S80 Tractor	Viceroy
DD 580	JHH 508N	DAF 2200 Tractor	Consul
DD 581	HAN 668N	DAF 2200 Tractor	Cyclone
DD 582	KRM 807P	DAF 2200 Tractor	Tornado
FD 583	KRM 968P	Foden S80 Tractor	Bandit
DD 584	LAO 731P	DAF 2200 Tractor	Kestrel
FD 585	LAO 871P	Foden S80 Tractor	Spartan
DD 586	LHH 493P	DAF 2200 Tractor	Rebel
DD 587	LRM 192P	DAF 2200 Tractor	Escort
FD 588	LRM 302P	Foden S80 Tractor	Roamer
DD 589	LRM 374P	DAF 2200 Tractor	Sceptre to 586
DD 590	LRM 971P	DAF 2200 Tractor	Falcon
DD 591	MAO 203P	DAF 2200 Tractor	Osprey
DD 592	MAO 835P	DAF 2200 Tractor	Wizard
DD 593	MHH 476P	DAF 2200 Tractor	Safari
FD 594	MRM 461P	Foden S80 Tractor	Jubilee
FD 595	LRG 422P	Ford Transit 4 wheel pick up	Valet
DD 596	NHH 604P	DAF 2200 Tractor	Saturn
DD 597	NHH 590P	DAF 2800 Tractor	Sultan
No information exists for fleet number 598			
DD 599	NRM 229P	DAF 2800 Tractor	Pullman
FD 600	NRM 302P	Foden S80 Tractor	Venture
FD 601	KSY 842J	Foden S39 Tractor	Wrangler
DD 602	ORM 272R	DAF 2800 Tractor	Viking
DD 603	PAO 30R	DAF 2800 Tractor	Majestic
DD 604	PAO 177R	DAF 2800 Tractor	Trophy
DD 605	PHH 60R	DAF 2800 Tractor	Crofter
DD 606	PHH 28R	DAF 2800 Tractor	Eclipse
DD 607	RAO 912R	DAF 2800 Tractor	Rocket
DD 608	RRM 577R	DAF 2800 Tractor	Defiant
DD 609	RRM 698R	DAF 2300 Tractor	Tempest
DD 610	SAO 363R	DAF 2300 Tractor	Sovereign
FD 611	SAO 245R	Foden S83 Tractor	Mercury
DD 612	SAO 502R	DAF 2800 Tractor	Norseman
DD 613	RHH 409R	DAF 2300 Tractor	Ensign
VD 614	XTY 193J	Volvo F86 Tractor	Repulse
FD 615	FHN 409J	Foden S39 Tractor	Tudor
DD 616	SRM 425R	DAF 2800 Tractor	Pegasus
VD 617	YNL 751H	Volvo F86 Tractor	Swallow

Fleet	Reg	Type	Name/Notes
VD 618	RNL 799G	Volvo F86 Tractor	Swift
FD 619	SAO 716G	Ford D1000 4 wheel tipper	Tipster Was 618; to 526
DD 620	SRM 456H	DAF 2200 Tractor	Curlew
VD 621	GNL 210L	Volvo F86 Tractor	Chequer
DD 622	TRM 284S	DAF 2300 Tractor	Maiden
DD 623	TRM 403S	DAF 2300 Tractor	Raven
DD 624	UAO 706S	DAF 2800 Tractor	Pageant
DD 625	UAO 692S	DAF 2300 Tractor	Tramper
FD 626	UAO 781S	Foden S83 Tractor	King
DD 627	UHH 140S	DAF 2800 Tractor	Trojan
DD 628	UHH 520S	DAF 2800 Tractor	Rover
DD 629	VAO 948S	DAF 2300 Tractor	Knight
FD 630	VHH 1S	Ford A Series pick up	Junior to 018
DD 631	VHH 801S	DAF 2300 Tractor	Captain
DD 632	VRM 61S	DAF 2300 Tractor	Airman
DD 633	WAO 259S	DAF 2300 Tractor	Hunter
DD 634	YHH 986K	ERF 'A' Tractor	Soldier
DD 635	PHH 759H	ERF 'A' Tractor	Sailor
DD 636	WHH 706S	DAF 2200 Tractor	Cowboy
DD 637	WHH 787S	DAF 2200 Tractor	Tinker
DD 638	DHH 371L	ERF 'A' Tractor	Meteor
DD 639	BHH 696L	ERF 'A' Tractor	Jester
DD 640	VHH 24J	ERF 'A' Tractor	Valour
FD 641	NHH 890M	Foden S80 Tractor	Melody
DD 642	WRM 841S	DAF 2300 Tractor	Trooper
DD 643	XAO 992S	DAF 2800 Tractor	Milkmaid/Druid
643	XHH 631S	DAF 2300 Tractor	Empress
No information exists for fleet number 644			
DD 645	YHH 618T	DAF 2800 Tractor	Mariner to 774
DD 646	YHH 701T	DAF 2300 Tractor	Swift to 775
DD 647	VUT 853J	ERF 4 wheel platform	Seagull
FD 648	VEH 784L	Ford 'D' 4 wheel platform	Druid
DD 649	XHH 197S	DAF 2300 Tractor	Trucker
DD 650	YRM 653T	DAF 2300 Tractor	Banner to 777
DD 651	AAO 846T	DAF 2300 Tractor	Nomad to 778
DD 652	AAO 964T	DAF 2300 Tractor	Roamer to 779
DD 653	AHH 155T	DAF 2300 Tractor	Pioneer to 780
654	HRM 772D	Land Rover	Bantam
DD 655	AHH 619T	DAF 2300 Tractor	Prefect to 781
FD 656	ARM 711T	Foden HM Tractor	Raider
DD 657	BAO 428T	Foden HM Tractor	Brigade
DD 658	BAO 513T	DAF 2800 Tractor	Yeoman to 783
FD 659	BAO 786T	Foden HM Tractor	Revenge to 784
FD 660	BAO 869T	Foden HM Tractor	Matador
FD 661	BRM 441T	Foden HM Tractor	Rapier to 786
FD 662	BRM 682T	Foden HM Tractor	Express to 787
FD 663	CHH 195T	Foden HM Tractor	Bulwark to 788
FD 664	CHH 834T	Foden HM Tractor	Tourist to 789
DD 665	CRM 115T	DAF 2800 Tractor	Dauphin to 790
DD 666	CRM 362T	DAF 2300 Tractor	Pennant to 791
DD 667	DAO 881T	DAF 2800 Tractor	Duchess to 792
668	OCE 562H	ERF 4 wheel platform	Dolphin
FD 669	DRM 1T	Foden HM Tractor	Clipper to 793
FD 670	DRM 50T	Foden HM Tractor	Mallard to 794
FD 671	ERM 721V	Foden HM Tractor	Governor to 795
DD 672	FAO 658V	DAF 2300 Tractor	Rambler to 796
DD 673	FAO 738V	DAF 2300 Tractor	Warrior to 797
674	NMS 915T	DAF 2300 Tractor	Sheriff to 798
675	NMS 916T	DAF 2300 Tractor	Laddie to 799
DD 676	NMS 917T	DAF 2300 Tractor	Lassie to 800
FD 677	FHH 901V	Foden HM Tractor	Courier to 801
678	GAO 610V	DAF 2300 Tractor	Panther to 802
FD 679	GAO 821V	Foden HM Tractor	Princess to 803
LD 680	GAO 858V	Leyland Clydesdale 4 wheel van	Sniper to 015
681	GHH 827V	Foden HM Tractor	Dragoon to 804
DD 682	GHH 925V	DAF 2300 Tractor	Dandy to 805
DD 683	EDP 779V	DAF 2300 Tractor	Countess to 806
No information exists for fleet numbers 684, 685 & 686			
ED 687	TEE 345J	ERF 4 wheel van	Bronco
LD 688	HRM 410V	Leyland Roadtrain Tractor	Patrol to 807
689	HRM 511V	DAF 2300 Tractor	Hussar to 808
FD 690	HRM 817V	Foden HM Tractor	Tycoon to 809
DD 691	DJH 480V	DAF 2800 Tractor	Patriot
692	DJH 478V	DAF 2300 Tractor	Baron
693	ECF 587V	DAF 2300 Tractor	Saxon to 810
ED 694	LWC 54J	ERF 4 wheel platform	Atlantis
DD 695	ECF 687V	DAF 2300 Tractor	Outlaw to 811
DD 696	DJH 479V	DAF 2300 Tractor	Marquis to 812
FD 697	LAO 811W	Foden HM Tractor	Monarch
DD 698	ELS 224W	DAF 2300 Tractor	Colleen
DD 699	MAO 568W	DAF 2800 Tractor	Citadel
DD 700	MAO 701W	DAF 2800 Tractor	Saracen
DD 701	MHH 902W	DAF 2800 Tractor	Romany
DD 702	MRM 63W	DAF 2800 Tractor	Tristar
DD 703	NAO 284W	DAF 2800 Tractor	Pilgrim
DD 704	NAO 429W	DAF 2800 Tractor	Griffin
FD 705	NHH 658W	Foden HM Tractor	Valiant
705	GWY 184N	Foden S80 Tractor	Conquest
FD 706	LAO 811W	Foden FM Tractor	Monarch
706	KWX 503P	Foden S80 Tractor	Minstrel
LD 707	RFC 944T	Leyland Sherpa Van	Hornet to 019
DD 708	NRM 515W	DAF 2800 Tractor	Maestro
FD 709	HMV 146N	Foden S80 Tractor	Robust
FD 710	HMV 147N	Foden S80 Tractor	Valour
DD 711	OAO 522W	DAF 2800 Tractor	Thistle
711	SVW 73M	Foden S80 Tractor	Tudor
DD 712	OAO 320W	DAF 2800 Tractor	Emblem
DD 713	OHH 247W	DAF 2800 Tractor	Sabre
DD 714	RAO 109X	DAF 2800 Tractor	Reaper
LD 715	RAO 659X	Leyland Roadtrain Tractor	Galaxy
715	HVD 646L	Albion 4 wheeled van	Badger
DD 716	RHH 79X	DAF 2800 Tractor	Fiesta
717	RHH 688X	DAF 2800 Tractor	Partisan
718	RRM 194X	Leyland Roadtrain Tractor	Mirage
719	SHH 202X	DAF 2800 Tractor	Sherpa
DD 720	SHH 272X	DAF 2800 Tractor	Bounty
DD 721	SHH 486X	DAF 2800 Tractor	Cougar
DD 722	SHH 523X	DAF 2800 Tractor	Artisan
723	SHH 458X	Ford A Series pick up	Rescue to 020
DD 724	THH 501X	DAF 2800 Tractor	Trident
FD 725	PPH 949R	Foden S80 Tractor	Ranger
726	VRM 431Y	DAF 2800 Tractor	Victory
DD 727	WAO 689Y	DAF 2300 Tractor	Hermes
DD 728	VAO 68Y	DAF 2300 Tractor	Cairn
728	TWY 510R	Foden S80 Tractor	Premier
729	TWY 511R	Foden S80 Tractor	Rogue
SD 730	YAO 528Y	Scania 112 Tractor	Legion
SD 731	YAO 529Y	Scania 112 Tractor	Harrier
732	EYS 680T	Seddon Atkinson 201 4 wheel platform	Badger to 017
732	A431 BHH	DAF 2800 Tractor	Champion
733	A434 BHH	DAF 2800 Tractor	Herald
734	A433 BHH	DAF 2800 Tractor	Prince
735	A435 BHH	DAF 2800 Tractor	Mustang
736	A436 BHH	DAF 2800 Tractor	Pirate
No information exists for fleet numbers 737, 738, 739 & 740			
741	NSX 319Y	ERF 'C' Tractor	Tartan
742	NSX 320Y	ERF 'C' Tractor	Chariot
No information exists for fleet numbers 743, 744 & 745			
FD 746	GSC 31T	Foden HM Tractor	Destiny
No information exists for fleet numbers 747, 748, 749 & 750			
751	GVA 395K	Scania 110 Tractor	Martin
752	A458 DAO	ERF 'C' Tractor	Mammoth Was 758
753	A459 DAO	ERF 'C' Tractor	Goliath Was 759
754	A386 NRO	DAF 2800 Tractor	Milkmaid/Migrant
755	A387 NRO	DAF 2800 Tractor	Queen
No information exists for fleet numbers 756, 757, 758, 759 & 760			
761	TRM 403S	DAF 2300 Tractor	Raven Was 623
No information exists for fleet numbers 762, 763, 764 & 765			
766	VHH 801S	DAF 2300 Tractor	Captain Was 631
No information exists for fleet numbers 767 & 768			
769	WHH 706S	DAF 2200 Tractor	Cowboy Was 636
No information exists for fleet number 770			
771	WRM 841S	DAF 2300 Tractor	Trooper Was 642
No information exists for fleet numbers 772 & 773			
774	YHH 618T	DAF 2800 Tractor	Mariner Was 645
775	YHH 701T	DAF 2300 Tractor	Swift Was 646
No information exists for fleet number 776			
777	YRM 653T	DAF 2300 Tractor	Banner Was 650

778	AAO 846T	DAF 2300 Tractor	Nomad Was 651
779	AAO 946T	DAF 2300 Tractor	Roamer Was 652
780	AHH 155T	DAF 2300 Tractor	Pioneer Was 653
781	AHH 619T	DAF 2300 Tractor	Prefect Was 655
		No information exists for fleet number 782	
783	BAO 513T	DAF 2800 Tractor	Yeoman Was 658
784	BAO 786T	Foden HM Tractor	Revenge Was 659
		No information exists for fleet number 785	
786	BRM 441T	Foden HM Tractor	Rapier Was 661
787	BRM 682T	Foden HM Tractor	Express Was 662
788	CHH 185T	Foden HM Tractor	Bulwark Was 663
789	CHH 834T	Foden HM Tractor	Tourist Was 664
790	CRM 115T	DAF 2800 Tractor	Dauphin Was 665
791	CRM 362T	DAF 2300 Tractor	Pennant Was 666
792	DAO 881T	DAF 2800 Tractor	Duchess Was 667
793	DRM 1T	Foden HM Tractor	Clipper Was 669
794	DRM 50T	Foden HM Tractor	Mallard Was 670
795	ERM 721V	Foden HM Tractor	Governor Was 671
796	FAO 658V	DAF 2300 Tractor	Rambler Was 672
797	FAO 738V	DAF 2300 Tractor	Warrior Was 673
798	NMS 915T	DAF 2300 Tractor	Sheriff Was 674
799	NMS 916T	DAF 2300 Tractor	Laddie Was 675
800	NMS 917T	DAF 2300 Tractor	Lassie Was 676
801	FHH 901V	Foden HM Tractor	Courier Was 677
802	GAO 610V	DAF 2300 Tractor	Panther Was 678
803	GAO 821V	Foden HM Tractor	Princess Was 679
804	GHH 827V	Foden HM Tractor	Dragoon Was 681
805	GHH 925V	DAF 2300 Tractor	Dandy Was 682
806	EDP 779V	DAF 2300 Tractor	Countess Was 683
807	HRM 410V	Leyland Roadtrain Tractor	Patrol Was 688
808	HRM 511V	DAF 2300 Tractor	Hussar Was 689
809	HRM 817V	Foden HM Tractor	Tycoon Was 690
810	ECF 581V	DAF 2300 Tractor	Saxon Was 693
811	ECF 587V	DAF 2300 Tractor	Outlaw Was 695
812	DJH 479V	DAF 2300 Tractor	Marquis Was 696
813	A560 EAO	DAF 2800 Tractor	Regent
814	A561 EAO	DAF 2800 Tractor	Century
815	A562 EAO	DAF 2800 Tractor	Centurion
816	A563 EAO	DAF 2800 Tractor	Citizen
817	A564 EAO	DAF 2800 Tractor	Knave
818	A565 EAO	DAF 2800 Tractor	Falcon
819	A866 EHH	Volvo F10 Tractor	Country
820	A867 EHH	Volvo F10 Tractor	Tudor
821	A868 EHH	Volvo F10 Tractor	Hawk
822	A121 JLS	Scania 112 six wheeled Tractor	Rebel
823	A34 SKX	DAF 2800 Tractor	Valour
824	A566 EAO	DAF 2800 Tractor	Heritage Was 819
825	A567 EAO	DAF 2800 Tractor	Bandit
826	A568 EAO	DAF 2800 Tractor	Osprey
827	A569 EAO	DAF 2800 Tractor	Tornado
828	A469 ONA	Scania 112 Tractor	Europa/Zeus
829	A570 EAO	DAF 2800 Tractor	Melody
830	A572 EAO	DAF 2800 Tractor	Ranger
831	A573 EAO	DAF 2800 Tractor	Amazon
832	A35 SKX	DAF 2800 Tractor	Merlin
833	B460 HAO	DAF 2800 Tractor	Bullet
834	B462 HAO	DAF 2800 Tractor	Cumbrian
835	B463 HAO	DAF 2800 Tractor	Hunter
836	B464 HAO	DAF 2800 Tractor	Aztec
837	B465 HAO	DAF 2800 Tractor	Student
838	B466 HAO	DAF 2800 Tractor	Graduate
839	B467 HAO	DAF 2800 Tractor	Steward
840	B468 HAO	DAF 2800 Tractor	Wizard
841	B469 HAO	DAF 2800 Tractor	Pegasus
842	B407 WBH	DAF 2800 Tractor	Consul
843	B408 WBH	DAF 2800 Tractor	Spartan
844	B116 LEM	Scania 112 Tractor	Sword
845	B117 LEM	Scania 112 Tractor	Juno
846	B409 WBH	DAF 2800 Tractor	Sultan
847	B118 LEM	Scania 112 Tractor	Utah
848	B119 LEM	Scania 112 Tractor	Omaha
849	B203 UND	Scania 112 Tractor	Gold
850	B204 UND	Scania 112 Tractor	Duke
851	B205 UND	Scania 112 Tractor	Renown
852	B206 UND	Scania 112 Tractor	Guise
853	B711 KAO	DAF 2800 Tractor	Deputy
854	B691 RLS	Scania 112 Tractor	Curlew
855	B692 RLS	Scania 112 Tractor	Scott
856	B693 RLS	Scania 112 Tractor	Piper
857	B694 RLS	Scania 112 Tractor	Grouse
858	B695 RLS	Scania 112 Tractor	Mogul
859	B696 RLS	Scania 112 Tractor	Hero
860	B697 RLS	Scania 112 Tractor	King
861	B712 KAO	DAF 2800 Tractor	Viking
862	B713 KAO	DAF 2800 Tractor	Trophy
863	B714 KAO	DAF 2800 Tractor	Rocket
864	B715 KAO	DAF 2800 Tractor	Sovereign
865	B716 KAO	DAF 2800 Tractor	Norseman
866	B717 KAO	DAF 2800 Tractor	Forester
867	B571 YGS	DAF 2800 Tractor	Ajax
868	B572 YGS	DAF 2800 Tractor	Macbeth
869	B573 YGS	DAF 2800 Tractor	Milkmaid
870	B574 YGS	DAF 2800 Tractor	Aegis
871	B575 YGS	DAF 2800 Tractor	Caesar
872	B576 YGS	DAF 2800 Tractor	Othello
873	B577 YGS	DAF 2800 Tractor	Claudius
874	B578 YGS	DAF 2800 Tractor	Adonis
875	C531 NFY	Scania 112 Tractor	Oak
876	C532 NFY	Scania 112 Tractor	Redwood
877	C647 HRN	Scania 112 Tractor	Beech
878	C648 HRN	Scania 112 Tractor	Birch
879	C649 HRN	Scania 112 Tractor	Aspen
880	C650 HRN	Scania 112 Tractor	Rowan
881	C651 HRN	Scania 112 Tractor	Laurel
882	C281 ORM	DAF 2800 ATi Tractor	Eden
883	C282 ORM	DAF 2800 ATi Tractor	Derwent
884	C283 ORM	DAF 2800 ATi Tractor	Solway
885	C264 PAO	ERF 'C' Tractor	Skiddaw
886	C265 PAO	ERF 'C' Tractor	Scafell
887	C266 PAO	ERF 'C' Tractor	Langdale
888	C326 YLS	Scania 112 Tractor	Tern
889	C327 YLS	Scania 112 Tractor	Forth
890	C328 YLS	Scania 112 Tractor	Clyde
891	C329 YLS	Scania 112 Tractor	Tay
892	C330 YLS	Scania 112 Tractor	Swan
893	C331 YLS	Scania 112 Tractor	Spey
894	C332 YLS	Scania 112 Tractor	Devon
895	C333 YLS	Scania 112 Tractor	Esk
896	C334 YLS	Scania 112 Tractor	Dee
897	D701 DMS	Scania 112 Tractor	Don
898	C336 YLS	Scania 112 Tractor	Islay
899	C201 HPP	DAF 2800 Tractor	Milkman
900	C202 HPP	DAF 2800 Tractor	Avon
901	C203 HPP	DAF 2800 Tractor	Milkround
902	C921 PAO	ERF 'C' Tractor	Coniston
903	C922 PAO	ERF 'C' Tractor	Uldale
904	C923 PAO	ERF 'C' Tractor	Caldew
905	C196 PHH	ERF 'C' Tractor	Teesdale
906	C197 PHH	ERF 'C' Tractor	Cheviot
907	C198 PHH	ERF 'C' Tractor	Kielder
908	E92 BAO	DAF 95 Tractor	Angler
909	E93 BAO	DAF 95 Tractor	Highlander
910	E94 BAO	DAF 95 Tractor	Sceptre
911	C443 HGS	Scania 112 Tractor	Cam
912	C444 HGS	Scania 112 Tractor	City
913	C445 HGS	Scania 112 Tractor	Ouse
914	C446 HGS	Scania 112 Tractor	Isis
		No information exists for fleet numbers: 915, 916 & 917	
918	E88 BHH	ERF 'E' Tractor	Eagle
919	E89 BHH	ERF 'E' Tractor	Valiant
920	E774 BHH	ERF 'E' Tractor	Rover
921	E775 BHH	ERF 'E' Tractor	Princess
922	E776 BHH	ERF 'E' Tractor	Poacher
923	E792 XFC	DAF 95 Tractor	Marquis
924	E506 BRM	DAF 95 Tractor	Sabre
925	E507 BRM	DAF 95 Tractor	Stuart
926	E508 BRM	DAF 95 Tractor	Mirage
927	E509 BRM	DAF 95 Tractor	Cougar

Fleet No.	Reg. No.	Type	Name
928	E510 BRM	DAF 95 Tractor	Lomond
929	E511 BRM	DAF 95 Tractor	Clansman
930	E512 BRM	DAF 95 Tractor	Galaxy
931	E505 BRM	DAF 95 Tractor	Colleen
999	B384 KAO	Mercedes Benz 1628 Tractor	Spitfire

SERVICE FLEET LIST

Fleet No.	Reg. No.	Type	Name
		No information exists for fleet numbers 001, 002, 003, 004, 005 & 006	
007	CHS 943X	Dodge Commando	
		No information exists for fleet numbers 008 & 009	
010	UMS 701T	Leyland Van	
011	EYS 681T	Seddon Atkinson 201 4 wheeler	Scout
		No information exists for fleet numbers 012, 013 & 014	
015	GAO 858V	Leyland Clydesdale 4 wheel van	Sniper Was 680
016	UGD 470W	Seddon Atkinson 201 4 wheel platform	Beaver Was 733
017	EYS 680T	Seddon Atkinson 201 4 wheel van	Badger Was 732
018	VHH 1S	Ford A Series pick up	Junior Was 630
019	RFC 944T	Leyland Sherpa Van	Hornet Was 707
020	SHH 458X	Ford A Series pick up	Rescue Was 723
021	MGA 95V	Ford 'D' 4 wheel curtainsider	Shuttle
		No information exists for fleet number 022	
023	B184 WBH	Bedford pick up	Revival
024	B686 LKD	Ford Escort van	
025	B881 RMS	Bedford pick up	Restorer
026	C140 DBA	Bedford van	
027	C623 OAO	Bedford van	Valet
028	C478 FNM	Bedford van	Response
029	C259 AMS	Bedford van	Remedy

UNITED GLASS ADDITIONS

Fleet No.	Reg. No.	Type	Name
567	SRX 3M	ERF 'B' Tractor	
576	GVA 398K	Scania 111 Tractor	Recovery
578	BDJ 477N	Scania 111 Tractor	
582	SNO 37M	ERF 'B' Tractor	Retriever
588	TTW 390N	Foden Tractor	
598	GBF 503N	Guy Big J Tractor	
623	PCF 841R	ERF 'B' Tractor	
627	VBY 928S	Foden Tractor	
628	XAN 18T	ERF 'B' Tractor	
629	YMO 692T	ERF 'B' Tractor	
630	YMO 693T	ERF 'B' Tractor	
631	AAN 612T	ERF 'B' Tractor	
632	PCP 505T	ERF 'B' Tractor	Condor
633	PCP 506T	ERF 'B' Tractor	Courage
634	PCP 507T	ERF 'B' Tractor	Consul
635	FUM 771T	Foden HM Tractor	
636	FUM 772T	Foden HM Tractor	Pageant
637	FUM 773T	Foden HM Tractor	Provost
638	FUM 774T	Foden HM Tractor	
		No information exists for fleet numbers 639, 640 & 641	
642	GSC 32T	Foden HM Tractor	
643	FFS 995T	Foden HM Tractor	Phoenix
644	CJM 741V	ERF 'B' Tractor	Master
645	CJM 742V	ERF 'B' Tractor	Mascot
646	XCX 398V	ERF 'B' Tractor	Viceroy
647	XCX 400V	ERF 'B' Tractor	Victor
648	KVX 265V	Foden HM Tractor	Charisma
649	KVX 266V	Foden HM Tractor	Talisman
650	GDJ 832V	Foden HM Tractor	Phantom
651	OSC 563V	ERF 'B' Tractor	Award
652	OSC 564V	ERF 'B' Tractor	Safari
653	OSX 701V	Foden HM Tractor	Acclaim
654	OSX 702V	Foden HM Tractor	Angler
655	JHJ 749V	ERF 'B' Tractor	Stallion
656	JHJ 748V	ERF 'B' Tractor	
657	CJM 752V	ERF 'B' Tractor	Salute
658	CJM 753V	ERF 'B' Tractor	Sapphire
659	CJM 754V	ERF 'B' Tractor	Spirit
660	GNE 386V	ERF 'B' Tractor	Lord

Fleet No.	Reg. No.	Type	Name
661	RFS 9V	ERF 'B' Tractor	Ochil
662	XCX 435V	ERF 'B' Tractor	Laird
663	XCX 436V	ERF 'B' Tractor	Venture
664	RFS 8V	ERF 'B' Tractor	Alien
665	RFS10V	ERF 'B' Tractor	Cyclone
666	RFS 12V	ERF 'B' Tractor	Eagle
667	RFS 13V	ERF 'B' Tractor	Castle
668	GDJ 821V	Foden HM Tractor	Pullman
669	GDJ 842V	Foden FM Tractor	Protector
670	GDJ 843V	Foden FM Tractor	Barbican
671	OSX 712V	Foden FM Tractor	Minstrel
672	OSX 713V	Foden FM Tractor	Arrow
673	OSX 714V	Foden FM Tractor	Highlander
674	OSX 715V	Foden FM Tractor	Clansman
675	KVS 279V	Foden FM Tractor	Superb
676	RVW 692W	ERF 'B' Tractor	Olympia
677	PMJ 889W	ERF 'B' Tractor	Scamp
678	LJP 829W	Foden HM Tractor	Bastion
679	OMS 943W	ERF 'B' Tractor	Conquest
680	OMS 944W	ERF 'B' Tractor	Stuart
681	SLK 830W	ERF 'B' Tractor	Saturn
682	GGM 37W	ERF 'B' Tractor	Squire
683	DFV 918W	ERF 'B' Tractor	Titan
684	LJP 837W	Foden FM Tractor	Diplomat
685	CGD 74X	Seddon Atkinson 401 Tractor	Flair
686	CGD 75X	Seddon Atkinson 401 Tractor	Charger
687	WLL 174X	ERF 'C' Tractor	Mighty
688	YBH 398X	DAF 2800 Tractor	Scorpion
689	KNS 624Y	Seddon Atkinson 401 Tractor	Envoy
690	KNS 625Y	Seddon Atkinson 401 Tractor	Elite
		No information exists for fleet numbers 691 & 692	
693	YCP 175Y	Seddon Atkinson 401 Tractor	Comet
694	YCP 176Y	Seddon Atkinson 401 Tractor	Cadet
695	YPA 335Y	Seddon Atkinson 401 Tractor	Glory
696	DNF 535Y	Scania 112 Tractor	Fox
697	A954 DAO	Volvo F10 Tractor	Javelin

UNKNOWN NUMBERS OR UNNUMBERED VEHICLES

Fleet No.	Reg. No.	Type	Name
	FT 5612	Bedford	Triumph
	JM 5692	Bedford	Hawk
	SW 7411	Bedford	Eagle
	XS 5572	Scammell R8 8 wheel platform	Empress ex BRS 63B250
		Foden	Master
	ABV 399	Albion	Clarion
	AGR 253	Bedford	Chief
	BCB 492	ERF	Lassie
	BEA 43	Foden	Supreme
	CTY 216	Bedford	Lady
		Bedford	Reaper
	DRR 159	Albion	Rover
	DTY 374	Bedford	Ensign/Major
	EHH 130	Leyland	Star
	EST 315	Albion	Viking
	FAO 199	Bedford	Clipper
	FED 106	Foden	Renown
	FWY 566	Albion	Minstrel
	GLG 88	ERF	Courier
	HAO 998	ERF	Emblem
	HHH 445	Ford	Legion
	HUP 600	Maudslay 4 wheel tractor	Ranger ex BRS 4D48
	JAO 919	Leyland	Panther
	KAO 51	Leyland	Airman
	KXW 606	Ford Thames 4 wheel platform	Linnet
	BEV 937B	Ford bonneted 4 wheel tractor	Trialist
	DUB 368C	Scammell Scarab 3 wheel Tractor	Bygone
	UHH 436J	Foden S39 Tractor	Nimrod
	UHH 616J	Foden S39 Tractor	Searcher
	TGD 517R	Seddon Atkinson 400 4 wheel Tractor	Melody
	TGD 520R	Seddon Atkinson 400 4 wheel Tractor	Drifter
	C217 HOJ	Leyland Roadtrain 4 wheel Tractor	Ophelia
	C218 HOJ	Leyland Roadtrain 4 wheel Tractor	Hamlet